Endors

"Eric's honest introspect reflects se...... .... law enforcement cultural norms that often negatively influence officers' emotional well-being. His profound anecdotes portray the hallmarks of so many feelings and emotions experienced by officers suffering in silence, and offers the reader a rare glance at influences that impede treatments. Eric's lived experiences, peer observations, and professional citations attest not only to the emotional truths and stigmas so many of us experiencing mental health challenges face, but also presents opportunities for others to notice, better understand, and intervene effectively. Eric provides proven approaches and resources that can make differences in so many lives. The consequences of an officer's reluctancy to pursue help and avoidance by others is necessarily imbedded in these pages, shadowed by pathways and powerful themes of hope, courage, and recovery. I offer not only my credible endorsement of this book's meaningful and impactful content, but also a living example of its potential to save lives. I'm not certain I would be alive to write this endorsement if not for Eric's application of this book's purpose in my life."

Capt. Joe Coffey (Ret) Warwick, RI Police Department
Former Capt. with Donald Wyatt Federal Detention Facility
Former SSGT, U.S. Army, Instructor, Rhode Island Military Academy

"I believe that any police officer, or the ones who love them, who read this book and are honest with themselves, will see themselves somewhere or what actually happens within the pages. The first step is recognizing there is an issue; the book will help to see oneself and while giving some direction for the next step. Eric Weaver looked and talked the part of a tough, no nonsense, by the book officer and ultimately the same type of sergeant. Eric was a leader on patrol and ETF (aka SWAT). It was crushing to learn about the pain Eric was really dealing with and still struggles with. However, I still see Eric as a leader; this time he is trying to save the life and soul of the officer from pain and suffering. "Greater love hath no man than this, that a man lay down his life for his friends." – John 15:13 Eric is laying (out) down his life for his friends!"

Capt. Mark Case (Ret) Rochester, NY Police Department

"Eric does a great job of providing insight from a true to life perspective. The bravery in publishing his stories adds to insight for others and furthers the de-stigmatization of an officer asking for help. The truth needs to be told. Law enforcement organizations need to learn from Eric's truth and provide mental health programs and services for their own officers. We need to know it is okay to love this job, know it takes its toll, and know our organization has our back."

Sgt. Kiersten Harzewski, New Mexico State Police.
CNT/CIT/POST

"This is one of the best books on First Responder Suicide Prevention and Wellness I have ever read. Those of us who have had the privilege to be taught by Eric Weaver or teach alongside him know how fortunate we are. His knowledge has helped me maintain my own emotional wellness and given me tools to look after those officers I work with, those who I supervise and most importantly, my family. One of the best things about Eric's book is the focus on families. That is going to be unbelievably impactful and help so many first responders and their families. I really haven't seen that in any other books or articles on first responder wellness. I thank God that Eric had the strength and courage to write this book from a lived experience perspective to let all First Responders know that no matter how bad they feel, recovery is possible."

Lt. Jeremy Romo, DSN 3126
St. Louis County Police Department
Bureau of Tactical Support

OVERCOMING THE DARKNESS

Shining Light on Mental Illness, Trauma, and Suicide in Law Enforcement

by Sgt. Eric Weaver (Ret.)

To contact the author, visit www.OvercomingtheDarkness.com

ISBN: 9780578755717

This book is dedicated to Officer Edwin Martinez and his family, in acknowledgement that his death was not in vain. It is also dedicated to the men and women of law enforcement and their families, in acknowledgement that their lives, in and outside of their careers, have true value and significance.

Exceptional Thank You and Acknowledgement

To my wife, Lynne, the true motivation and inspiration behind my continued recovery and completion of this book, and who, along with God, has kept me alive.

To my three daughters, Erika, Danielle, and Samantha, who have lived through and have experienced my journey, good and bad, and whom I love very much.

Special Thanks:

Kathy Palokoff, Editor
Founder and Chief Igniter
www.gofirestarter.com

Clinical Advisors:

Renae Carapella-Johnson LMHC, NCC
Ray of Light Counseling and Consulting
www.mightyrayoflight.com

Shirin Boose, M.Ed., LPCC-S
Rising Tide Counseling and Consulting
www.risingtidecle.com

Ingrid Wander, LCSW-R

Karen B. Dudgeon, LCSW

Kynna Murphy, LCSW-R, MSW

TABLE OF CONTENTS

INTRODUCTION

When I first started writing *Overcoming the Darkness,* my audience was clear. I was writing for my fellow colleagues in law enforcement – the officers and their supervisors who keep our world safe and often pay a high price for fulfilling their duty. We often think of that price in terms of physical loss. What has been clear to me over the years is that the price is as equally steep, if not even more so, mentally and emotionally.

My intention was to give a raw accounting of my own experiences, coupled with knowledge gained from 20 years of teaching literally thousands of officers in all aspects of law enforcement about suicide, trauma, and mental illness. My classes have included:

- Local and State police departments
- Local and State corrections staff
- Military police
- Federal agencies
- 911 dispatch staff
- College and university police
- Private security employees
- Court Security and staff
- Probation and parole
- Hostage Negotiators
- EMS staff

The challenges of mental illness, trauma, and suicide go far beyond those people directly involved. There are more than 800,000 sworn law enforcement officers[1] and almost 500,000 corrections officers[2] in the United States. Do a low estimate that each officer has ten people in their immediate circle – husbands, wives, fathers, mothers, sons, daughters, sisters, and brothers, and close friends – who are impacted by their life. Those are thirteen million people who are potentially affected by what their loved ones working in law enforcement experience. As you might imagine, that number of people is on the low side.

Now take it out to the broader population. Almost 46 million Americans experience mental illness[3], and over 48,000 die by suicide[4] in a given year. Two hundred and twenty-three million have experienced some type of traumatic event at least once in their lifetime[5]. That's a lot of hurting people.

As you read this book, you will see that while most of my stories and examples are centered on law enforcement, the information is relevant to their families and countless other emergency services professions.

So many of us are challenged with overcoming the darkness in our lives. With cries of defunding police, the attacking of our profession, and so many other factors in our society, we often forget or put aside our emotional well-being. I believe with all my heart that law enforcement is a very noble and honorable profession, and it is my deep hope that this book will shine light on what your family, friends and community may be facing and provide a new path forward. Most importantly, if you are personally experiencing mental illness, cumulative stress, trauma, or suicidal thoughts, know that you are not alone. I, along with other individuals, resources, and organizations throughout our great country, am here to help you. It is my sincere desire that this book is one of those resources.

- Sgt. Eric Weaver (Ret)

CHAPTER 1

DARKNESS OF THE HEART AND SOUL

I had never seen anyone die before. Now I stood staring up at a young man hanging from the door frame of his jail cell. It was 1983. I was 20 years old and it was Thanksgiving night. I had only been on the job for six weeks. My 17-year-old wife was at home with our baby, because I had volunteered to work over-time that night. We needed the money.

Because it was a holiday, the cell block was really quiet with the inmates watching football on TV. I was at the officer's station on the second floor where the isolation and observation cells were also located. The observation cell was for those at a little higher risk, but it was not a 24hr. watch kind of cell. It was made of tempered glass, and where it was placed on the floor was horrifically designed. Sitting in the guard office, you would be able to look down the dayroom hallway, but you could only see half of the cell. So, unless you physically walked down the hallway, you wouldn't be able to see the other half unless you walked around the corner toward one of the other isolation cells. So, I would do my routine walk around the cell blocks and dayrooms. Nothing was out of the ordinary, so the third-floor deputy came down to my floor and we sat talking during our breaks.

"Time to do a check," I said. I began walking down the hall of day rooms, and as I rounded the corner to see the other half of the cell I couldn't see from the officer's station, this young man, who was a nice kid who I had talked with previously during the day, was hanging with a sheet around his neck with his eyes looking right at me. He was gray and lifeless. I called down to control because they had to unlock the door from Main Control. The door unlocked; I yelled for the other deputy to help; and we got him down.

I remember getting the sheets off around his throat and trying to recall some CPR or first aid. I knew I must have learned it during a PE class in my short year at college, so I just started doing whatever CPR and mouth-to-mouth that made sense.

Let me be brutally honest. The incredibly sad but real truth is that I wasn't trying to be a hero and save this young man from dying. I didn't really know him and was certainly not personally involved in his life. Admittedly, here's what was going through my head: "What the fuck? I'm going to lose my job. It's my responsibility, and this kid is dead. I'm going to get fired and I can't let it happen. What am I going to do? Where am I going to work?"

I certainly didn't voice those thoughts, but they were running on a track in my mind as I tried CPR. I felt I was doing everything wrong. I couldn't remember the right order, or anything about airway/breathing/compressions. I was just blowing in his stomach instead of his lungs, and he was vomiting in my mouth. It was just nasty—the taste of his last meal and the bitter bile in my mouth. All I wanted was to keep him alive until the ambulance got there so he didn't die on my shift. Finally, the paramedics got him stabilized and took him to the hospital. I don't remember going home when my shift ended at 11 p.m. I don't remember filing a report. I don't remember anything that happened after the ambulance left.

I talked with my wife after the incident. But she was 17 and a new mom. I probably told her what happened and that was it.

This was 1983, and the word, "debrief" didn't even exist back then. You just told people what happened. Nobody – including my wife – asked me what I was feeling as his vomit filled my mouth while I desperately tried to get him to breathe. So, I just told the facts and reassured her that I didn't think I was going to be fired.

There was no mention of my fear or guilt. I remember coming in the next day, getting pats on the back, and everyone looking at me like I had done something really good. I didn't feel like I deserved anything. I questioned whether it was my fault because maybe I should have checked on him sooner. He was my responsibility, and even though I had saved his life, I felt as though I blew it. I also felt guilty because I was thinking about losing my job, while somebody's son and brother was dying.

The young man lived, and I got a life-saving award during a ceremony at the American Legion. Now I added another emotion to the swirling cauldron that was going on inside me. I was angry because the other officer who was there during the suicide attempt also got an award. All I could think was: "Why did you get one? You were terrified. You were scared to death and out of your mind. You didn't do a damn thing." How incredibly stupid and selfish of me. Once again, this was what was going on in my head. Nobody knew because I kept my mouth shut.

Today, I know that guilt, anger, and fear are all normal after a traumatic event. More importantly, after working with thousands of corrections and law enforcement officers, I know that the unbearable and lonely silence we exist in *is not normal*. This silence draws officers into the darkness, acting like a magnet for anxiety and depression.

Three days after the suicide attempt, I felt a deep need to do something. At that time, I didn't recognize it as a need for closure. Absence of closure is something I talk about often as I lecture around the country. It is one of the core causes of cumulative stress and trauma, which we will talk about in-depth in this book.

What does absence of closure look like? Often, law enforcement officers have situations where they deal with victims and have no actual interaction with them later on. You can spend hours with a rape victim and never see her again. You can spend days with kids who have been abused and never find out what happened. You simply have no idea what occurs once they're out of your sight. There is no closure and—like silence – it creates a hole in your soul and heart that often gets filled in destructive ways.

So unknowingly seeking closure, I asked my senior corrections officer if I could spend my shift at the hospital watching the kid whose life I had saved. Even though he was at the hospital, he was still an inmate, so somebody had to guard him 24 hours a day. "Are you sure you want to do that?" he asked. "Yeah," I answered. "I need to see him alive."

When I got to the hospital he was lying in the bed. I didn't show it, but I was relieved, pissed, sad, and angry all at the same time. Then the parents came in and started yelling about how we had killed their son. They didn't know that I was the guy who saved his life. And believe me they never knew – and will never know—what it has taken me decades to admit. I didn't save his life so they would get their son back. I saved his life to save my job—100 percent. I'm not proud of that, but it's the truth.

This first trauma was the beginning of darkness entering my heart and soul. Two years into that job, at 22 years old, I became a police officer in Rochester, NY, a relatively urban environment. I joined a culture of silence where being tough inside and out was the only way to fit in. I joined a world where rape, murder, violence, abuse, and every inhumanity that men and women could face and perpetuate happened daily.

My time as a corrections officer started me on the road to darkness, but my decision to become a police officer jumpstarted the post-traumatic stress—that continual pounding of stressful events and traumas over and over and over again. It cost me two marriages, and nearly cost me my career, my family and my life. And it took me many years to realize that I was not alone as I witnessed the devastating effect that cumulative stress and trauma were having on my fellow officers.

The law enforcement profession has an incredibly high percentage of undiagnosed PTSD, suicide, divorce, addictions, and untreated mental illness. What is going on? It is my belief – and those of other experts – that these problems arise out of complex, cumulative trauma, which is on-going trauma that finally causes an individual to reach their breaking point.

Today my mission is to let both law enforcement and the general public know that the staggering rates of Post-Traumatic Stress Disorder (PTSD) among corrections and police officers are often caused by cumulative stress and continual and complex trauma – not just a single incident.

Ironically, while law enforcement agencies have come a long way in recognizing and treating trauma, the focus is often still on police-involved shootings. If you're involved in a shooting, most departments have automatic debriefings. There are certain policies and procedures that the department puts in place for the good of the officers involved. But here's the reality: Like myself, the vast majority of officers will go through their entire career without being involved in an actual shooting incident, or ever even discharge their weapon. Yet, all of us will face countless other types of trauma during our 20, 25, or 30-year career.

At this point, you might be thinking, "Come on, Eric. Every job has its dark side. What makes cops so different? Maybe you were just a sensitive guy." Let me assure you, I was not a sensitive guy. I was tough. Nobody messed with me. I was also a leader – a police sergeant who commanded the respect of my officers.

Was I a good cop? It depends on whom you ask. If you ask the hundreds of people I've arrested, they may say no. If you ask the thousands of crime victims and mentally ill individuals I've helped, they'd probably say yes. If you ask the people I've arrested after raiding a drug house, they would again, probably say no. But if you ask the people who had to live and raise their families next to that drug house, they would probably say yes. I guess the question of 'good cop' all depends on one's perspective.

In my 20-year career in Rochester, I worked the toughest and most violent sections of a city. When you drive around those streets at 2 a.m. in the morning, you are responding to shots fired, shootings, domestic disputes, fights, and stabbings. You just go from one call to another call to another call, seeing death and destruction, hardship and poverty all along the way. And then you do it again the next day.

Let me tell you about a day in the life of a police officer. A typical day can literally range from family troubles to neighbor problems, to barking dogs, to fights with knives, to fights with guns, to shots fired, to a house fire, to a traffic stop, to another family trouble, to another neighbor problem, to a parking complaint, to another customer dispute. You respond to a fight with youths with bats and sticks. A girlfriend needs to retrieve property from her boyfriend's house and doesn't want to get beat up for being there. There's somebody with a knife on the corner. Then somebody drives away from the gas station without paying. Over and over and over. Your day covers such a wide variety of things.

When I train police officers, I often say that we actually do have a very monotonous job. We might respond to fights and shootings and run our asses ragged for eight hours, but a lot of it is pretty much the same thing over and over every day. This monotony can make us cold. It's just another shooting, another whatever. Our level of empathy starts to get weighted down. You get colder and colder. The darkness seeps in. But you don't even see it coming. The cumulative stress and trauma is like fog that surrounds you. You know that you're not seeing quite right, but you just keep on driving on.

For many officers, empathy gets eroded when you are mostly only dealing with the people who really don't like you or are victimized. It is rare to encounter the 80% of the population that supports the police and actually wants us to do our job. Real life is not like a television show where the police officers are heroes. What happens in reality is that we rarely see those people who respect and honor us. You rarely ever see the people who say, "You're doing a great job." Whoever says that to us? We're on a 911 call because somebody is drunk and a girlfriend and her kids just got beat up by her boyfriend. Nobody in that situation is going to be singing our praises.

The people that like and support the police? We know they are there, but we don't ever really get to see them because they are the silent majority trying to survive in a hostile environment, sometimes hiding in their homes or not living in the places where you work. We see the people that are supportive once in a blue moon, at a little thing like a festival or something. You'll have someone come up to you and go, "Oh, thank you officer," "Thank you for doing your job, officer," "Thank you for your work," "Thank you for your service." Every once in a while, you get one of those, but that's a relatively rare and special occasion.

You get the moms and dads who when you walk by, just grab their kids and say, "If you're not good, I'm going to have the officer take you to jail." I've heard this about a bazillion times. What do you think it does to the kids growing up? It makes them scared of the police. It makes them believe that the police are not their friends. I've had five-year-olds give me the finger at the encouragement of their parents.

That's the way I lived. It seemed like I lived in a world where it felt like people either fear or hate the police. How many people get nervous just because a police car pulls up behind them at a red light, even though you've done nothing wrong? And, if I'm kicking in a crack house door, it's hard to think that anyone is happy, except of course, the neighbors who have to live next door. This begins to change and affect how you feel about people in general.

Over the years, I started to really dislike people...a lot. When I was suicidal in 1996 and 1998, and for many years before, the person I hated the most was me. It wasn't until the year 2000, when I became a Christian and started looking at people in different ways, that my job got a lot easier. But until then, I disliked everybody and was angry about everything and at everyone.

Can law enforcement officers ever avoid the violence, abuse, and hate that happens every day no matter where in the community? Of course not. It comes with the job. But changing how we treat cumulative stress, depression, anxiety, substance use, and trauma can absolutely reduce the skyrocketing mental illness and suicide rates among my brothers and sisters who protect and serve, and the families they live with. In the next chapter, I'd like to give you an insider view of becoming a law enforcement officer.

CHAPTER 2

THE MAKING OF A LAW ENFORCE-MENT OFFICER

"Firsts" in our lives are important. The first day of school. The first kiss. The first love. The first time you see your child. The first day on a job. Sometimes, these firsts are filled with joy. Sometimes, they are indicators of upcoming trouble. I remember two important firsts—my first day working in the jail as a corrections officer, and the day I started working as a police officer—two very different places and environments.

On my first day working as a corrections officer as a 20-year-old kid in September of 1983, I was scared to death and didn't know what to expect. I walked into that secure environment, passing jail cells and cell blocks filled with people who had committed crimes. This was the first time I had seen people in jail. Ontario County Jail in upstate Canandaigua, New York at that time was a small jail, holding around 100 inmates. When you first walked in, you went down to the basement for roll call where you found out who was on the shift and who was going to be the senior correction officer that day. You would then take the elevator upstairs to the booking area and central control.

Central control was a good-sized room that had all the computers and video cameras as well as the buttons to secure doors.

There was a glass holding cell where people were put when they got arrested as well as a fingerprinting desk. I would take an elevator up to the cell blocks. There were 10 to 15 cells in each cell block. Some were empty, but most often the place was full. There was also an observation cell and other isolation cells. Juveniles were kept on a different floor.

County jails are pretty much maximum security, because a lot of people in there are waiting to go to trial for murder and other violent crimes. From my first day, I felt that it was us against them. That was clearly the attitude of all the corrections officers. We felt that we were better than the inmates because if you were in jail, you were obviously not a good person. At 20 years old, that feeling seemed natural. I also felt important. I was wearing a uniform, and for someone with low self-esteem, I felt like I was actually in charge of something.

As the days progressed, I started learning my job. One thing I didn't think about before I started working, was how tough it would be to be locked in for an entire shift. You couldn't go anywhere, even for lunch. You were in jail just like the inmates. You got to leave at the end of the day, but you were still in jail for over eight hours a day.

It was very different, but you assimilated into the system the best you could. One of my weirdest moments was the first time I had to search somebody. Obviously when you search people in jail, it's not just patting them down. They're taking off their underwear and bending over in front of you. It gets very personal. That was an experience that I never really thought about before.

Because I was new, I was under a great deal of scrutiny by both the people who worked there and the inmates. Essentially, you assimilated and learned your job really fast, or you didn't. If you didn't, you were marked and ridiculed by not only the inmates, but by your fellow deputies. I knew I had to fit into the culture of the people that I worked with. I knew that if I did not become "one of the boys" immediately, I would be ostracized quickly. Later on in my career, I would learn more about what becoming one of the boys meant in terms of mental and emotional health.

So, you grew up really fast. I went from working part time jobs at a Ponderosa Steakhouse, flipping hamburgers and steaks, and as a security guard at a local community college to having a job where I had real authority over people. I could legally take their rights away and lock them up in cells. You were not only responsible for other people, but also for *everything* that went on with them. This was not a job for a young man; it was a job for a grown man. I had just gotten married, was a new father and was trying to learn this new job. I didn't have any real-life experience in anything.

At this point, I needed to act, behave, and talk in certain ways. The tougher you were, the better you fit in. I swore hardly at all before I became a sheriff's deputy. Then I was swearing up a storm because that's just what you did to fit in. You yelled at people a lot. If you had to use force, you did and didn't think twice about it. Simply, you had to assimilate really fast, but you had to do it wisely.

I remember one kid who started with me. He tried to fit in by acting like an asshole, but he was such an asshole to everybody that even his fellow deputies hated him. He got fired. Then there was another kid who was a pushover, couldn't make decisions very well, and was too nice. Both deputies and inmates made fun of him, and he got fired. I assimilated by finding a balance and saying the right things to get liked by people, but not *too* liked.

In the beginning, I saw the inmates as people. Overtime, it became harder. When you're dealing with inmates who are fighting and spitting at you, your attitude changes really fast. But then again, you're bringing people medication, letting them make phone calls to their girlfriends, and taking them down to visitation. I think that when you're in there locked up with them for so long, you start seeing them more as people again. A lot of how you felt had to do with the individual. Some inmates were just mean, nasty, and rotten people, others were actually pretty nice.

One of the things I was known for was giving inmates haircuts before they had to go to court. We didn't have a barber, but we had scissors and clippers. When I would cut their hair, I would have conversations with them. I remember this one man who killed both his mother and father with an ax. Before a court appearance, he asked if he could have a haircut. I took him out of his cell and put him on the third-floor landing. Here I was, all by myself cutting the hair of a guy who had just murdered his parents with an ax. I should have gotten into a lot of trouble for that, but nobody said anything. They figured I knew what I was doing. This guy was actually a really super nice guy with mental health problems, who hated his parents. I felt no threat from him whatsoever.

On one occasion, it got quite personal. When I was in junior high school, three older kids robbed me in the school hallway after band practice. They grabbed me, took money out of my pockets, and slapped me around. I ran home and didn't tell anyone. Fast-forward six years and I am making my rounds around the cell block. There were two of the kids who robbed me. I didn't say a word and they didn't say a word, but there was a lot spoken. It felt really good.

I left my job at the jail to become a police officer. It was all I wanted to do. I think a difference in police officers versus "regular people" is the desire to really want to help people. When I first joined the police department back in 1985 with the city of Rochester, one of the first interview questions was, "Why do you want to be a cop?" Most people say they want to help people, and that's honestly how I felt. I wanted to be involved in changing people's lives. I also wanted to arrest bad guys and uphold the law and be the proverbial crime fighter.

There are some people who chose law enforcement just because they need a job. That doesn't generally work out too well. You need to do it because you want to do it. If I was doing it just because I needed a paycheck, I wasn't going to last very long because the culture doesn't allow that. Your heart must be in it. There's also an aspect of the uniform, the culture, and belonging to a group. It's very similar to the military—the feeling of belonging to something bigger than you and being part of a brotherhood and sisterhood.

A person's background, childhood, and personality also play a big role in why someone would become a cop. As I mentioned, I grew up with incredibly low self-esteem. I got beat up in school and pushed down in the mud. I was this short, fat kid who wasn't allowed to play sports. So, I asked myself, "What profession can I do where people have to do as I say? Where people have to listen to me? When I get to wear a badge and drive a fast car? Where people won't make fun of me and push me around anymore?" I remember going to the New York State Fair in Syracuse, New York with my family when I was a boy. All I wanted to do was hang around the state trooper's exhibit. Later on in my early teens, I joined the Police Explorer Program.

I became a cop so I would feel like I was somebody as well as help people. Today when I talk about understanding human distress and recognizing low self-esteem, I have asked thousands of police officers, "Do you think Eric Weaver is the only person who ever became a cop to self-medicate his or her low self-esteem?" The answer of course is, "No." But we're not the only profession that does that. I remember having an open conversation with a doctor once who admitted that the only reason he became a doctor was so people would call him 'doctor.'

Here's what I tell people when I am invited to speak: "I hate guns. I was never a hunter. I never hunted as a kid. Why did I eventually join the SWAT team and later become a sniper? Here's the truth. I joined so I could tell people that I'm a sniper on

SWAT and they would go, 'Wow, that's awesome.' My self-esteem would go, 'Yes. Look at me.'" This is also the same reason I competed in bodybuilding shows, had affairs, and did a plethora of other stupid things, just so I could feel better about myself.

When I became a police officer, I was in a better position than some people, because I had two years of jail experience dealing with people in very difficult situations. I knew how to talk to people better than officers who go on the street right out of college without any experience dealing with people that way. But regardless, I felt the exact same pressure and need to fit in that I had experienced in the jail.

The police academy setting wasn't necessarily real life; it was all classroom stuff. It all really started with field training where experienced officers evaluated you. My first field-training officer was not a nice person. His training method was to make you feel inadequate. I got yelled at constantly and was even smacked with a nightstick once.

My most memorable experience during field training was on a day it had just rained, and a big puddle had accumulated under a bridge. I apparently made the 'unforgivable' mistake of driving around the puddle instead of driving through it and splashing a pedestrian. My field training officer literally hit me for that "offense." "What do you think you're doing? Do you see that puddle?" he yelled. "You never go around a fucking puddle. You just fucking splash him." He made up nonsense about something else just so he could give me a low mark for driving that day on my daily observation report. He also made me arm-wrestle a bar owner in front of a crowd of about 100 people. I was ready to quit. "If this is what it's like, I can't and don't want to do this." I told my soon-to-be second wife. "I'm going to quit." At the police academy I was a platoon leader, but in field training I felt like nothing. But this was now my job, so I didn't leave. It was the only thing I knew how to do; it was the only thing I wanted to learn how to do. I never even considered not being a cop.

I quickly realized that in field training, you were making a reputation for yourself. The reputation could be a good or bad one. A good reputation meant you were tough, could fight, and didn't put up with any nonsense. A bad reputation meant you were weak, backed off from a fight, and couldn't hold your ground. If you had a bad reputation, you were ostracized immediately and never made it through training, and even if you did, no one wanted to work with you.

Being out on my own after field training was a hard-earned gift. I could learn from my mistakes and do things my way. Unfortunately, I became who my career wanted me to be really quickly. I certainly wasn't the nicest guy in the world. And when I became a field-training officer, I regrettably did much of the same things to my recruits that were done to me.

Everybody thought it was just what you did; there were not a whole lot of other options. If I wanted to have friends and be 'one of the boys', I had to be part of the culture. Without being one of the boys, I was not going to make it. My shift would be hard because no one would want to talk to me or back me up. No one would want to go on a call with me. When your life can easily be in someone else's hands, you do and say things that you probably wouldn't normally do. I saw first-hand how officers who were not one of the boys were treated, and I didn't want any part of that.

I was a pretty typical cop at that time. Of course, not everyone, but many of the cops I knew had affairs. That's just what we did because it was easily accessible, allowed, and almost expected of you. When it came to force, you did what you needed to do. It's amazing how much the general public doesn't realize how difficult it can be to handcuff someone who doesn't want to be handcuffed. Force is necessary when there's resistance, as long as it wasn't done excessively. You did what you had to do sometimes just to survive. But, we self-medicated a lot with alcohol, sex, pornography, and all that kind of stuff to escape life anyway we could. These are issues that I will delve into much deeper as I go on.

I think the culture is better now, but the culture is still the culture. Even today when I share this perspective with police officers in my classes, they respond by saying that it is still that way quite a bit. What has changed is how we treat people. Today's police officers are much more apt to talk to somebody as opposed to just grabbing them. But the law enforcement culture is not a culture that evolves very quickly.

One of things changing at a snail's pace is the view that law enforcement officers must be almost invincible. It is like "real men don't cry" on steroids. Here's the truth: You do need to be tough in the moment. You can't just run off and start crying because you see a dead child. You've got to do what you've got to do. The majority of people in law enforcement think you need to be tough all of the time. That's just not true. I didn't need to be tough after an incident was over, but unfortunately, I would often take toughness and bring it outside of work. I brought it home with me. We take it out on our spouses, our kids and on each other. I'll cover that in the chapter on family.

I, like most officers, dealt with trauma by telling war stories. I tell you what I did and then you tell your story and then another guy tells his story. And we add humor. We call it cop or gallows humor. Here's an example; I went to a motor vehicle accident. It was a motorcyclist who got decapitated. I said, "Lost his head over that one, didn't he?" With stories and laughter, we keep re-traumatizing each other. When I have asked people in my training classes why we do this, the response is always the same: "That's how we relieve stress." I'll address that at length later as well. By the way, this is not just a cop thing. Nurses do it, ambulance drivers do it, as do many other professions that deal with tragedy.

I remember responding to one of my first suicide scenes in 1986 that came in as a 'shots fired' call in a townhouse complex.

As I entered the main door, I looked up the stairs to the second floor. The apartment door was open, and all I could hear was a baby crying. I slowly walked up the stairs, stepping over blood and bone fragments. As I got to the door with my weapon drawn, I saw a heavy-set man slouched under the kitchen table, head blown in half. He killed himself while his baby was in the other room. It was Christmas time with decorations scattered about, as well as a plate of Christmas cookies sitting on the table right where the man had shot himself. I don't think I need to go into detail as to what was covering that plate of cookies.

As I'm contacting the medical examiner's office and trying to find out who's coming to take care of this baby, my lieutenant arrived on the scene. While I was briefing him, he went over and picked up the tray of cookies. He looked directly at me and laughed: "Hey Eric, want some cookies?" I laughed back and said, "No, thank you." What my lieutenant didn't know was that one of my family members died by suicide in the same way a couple years back. Do you think I told him that? Of course not. I just laughed and said, "That's a good one, Lieutenant."

I tell this story because even though I rarely remember what I had for dinner the last night, I can recall exactly my lieutenant's expression, that room, and those stupid cookies like it was 60 seconds ago. That's how we 'relieve stress'. Great stress reliever for my lieutenant, but it burned an image in my brain that will never leave.

When it comes to cop humor relieving our stress, I ask people in my classes, "How is that working for us?" Because if it worked, we would not see the high suicide, alcoholism, trauma and domestic violence rates among law enforcement. If just telling war stories and talking about our trauma to each other worked, my class would be four minutes long. We've been trying to make that work for 200 years, ever since Sir Robert Peel invented policing. It just doesn't work and it's killing us. That's one thing we really need to change.

I started out this chapter talking about "firsts." I wish I could tell you the first time I recognized that I was having deep emotional and mental issues dealing with the trauma of being a police officer. I can't. What I can tell you is that by the time I found out, it was almost too late. And even then, all I really cared about was keeping silent about what was going on. Being one of the boys was that important to me. Now let's explore the cost of that silence.

CHAPTER 3

THE COST OF SILENCE

Nobody knew the toll that trauma was having on my life, especially me. In 1992 I got promoted to sergeant in a 700-person department. It was a big deal to me. I spent five years on a SWAT team as a training coordinator. I taught our SWAT guys how to be SWAT guys. I was a sniper. I was in charge of a platoon of officers that was wiping narcotics off the streets. It was all very cool, and I was getting the job done.

Nothing out of ordinary was happening in my everyday life at home or at work. But I noticed around 1995 that suddenly I was feeling real shame and guilt over some of my stupid behaviors and choices in the past, both personal and professional. I would go to work and show strength and fortitude; no one had a clue that I was actually feeling bad about anything. Then the negative obsessive thinking started about so many things, both personally and professionally. So, I started self-medicating my anxiety, guilt, and shame. This led to thoughts of suicide, and I started acting even tougher and rougher. I put the SWAT guys through hell—literally through hell—because I needed to feel good. But inside, I was like, "Oh my gosh...What is happening to me?"

These feelings were overwhelming; it was the beginning of my obsessive-compulsive disorder (OCD). People think OCD is just about non-stop washing of your hands. It is far more complex and extends into many parts of your life. With obsessive-compulsive disorder, you have your compulsions, obsessions, thoughts, and then compulsions to act upon those thoughts. One of my compulsions, for example, is to make sure that I always check in with everybody to make sure everything is okay. "I'm not in trouble, right? You're not mad at me, are you?" It can be severe and disabling.

Then one day I went home and had a conversation with my wife.

"I need to tell you something, but you need to promise you don't tell anybody about this."

"Sure, what is it?"

"I can't stop thinking of killing myself."

"We've got to tell somebody."

"You don't tell anybody about this."

"You've got to get some help."

"Fine, I'll get some help but no one's going to learn about this because do you have any idea of what people would say?"

When I reflect back on that conversation, it wasn't like I woke up one day and wanted to kill myself. Things were starting to pop up in my mind and obsessive guilt started, combined with emotional exhaustion, cumulative stress, and trauma. It felt to me that suicide seemed like an option. And then suicide slowly became the only option for me. I had no idea the severity of it. When I told her that I wanted to kill myself, I was just having a conversation. I had no idea the impact that would lead to nine hospitalizations and several near suicide attempts over 24 years.

There were many reasons why I just didn't kill myself and instead told my wife. Today, I think God had a lot to do with it.

There was part of me that wanted to die, and there was part of me that wanted to live. And the part of me that wanted to live was still a little bit stronger than the part of me that wanted to die. I will talk about this – suicidal ambivalence – more in the chapter on Suicide.

So, I went to my primary care doctor and explained a little bit about what was going on. Not once did I mention I was suicidal, and back then, most doctors never thought of even asking. She sent me to a psychologist, which was a very strange experience for me because I never told anyone really what I was feeling. I started talking about a few of my issues, challenges and traumas. It was not enough.

In the spring of 1996 – ironically 10 years after I had gone on my first suicide call as a police officer—I was hospitalized because my thoughts of suicide were so intense. I knew that I needed more help, or I would take my life. But even feeling this desperate, it was vitally important to me to maintain my persona of strong Sergeant Eric Weaver.

Before I went to the hospital, I called in sick to work as required. Do you think I said, "Hey, this is Sergeant Weaver. Listen, I'm not coming to work today because I'm thinking about killing myself?" Of course not. If you know anything about police officers, I knew the second I hung up that phone, thirty other phones would start ringing with the news. Police officers, like all of us, love a good piece of gossip.

Instead, I told the officer at headquarters that I was working out, doing squats, and my back went out. A couple of years prior, I had back surgery, so I figured it wouldn't be questioned. His response? "All right. That's cool. Hope you're ok." There's no stigma around getting hurt exercising. As a matter of fact, it sounded pretty macho. In reality, I was going to a psychiatric hospital. It was a very surreal experience. Here I was, this tough SWAT sergeant, and they were taking my shoelaces away.

After a week, the hospital told me I was doing well and could go back home, but to stay out of work. I remember being advised to get some hobbies. A week later, I barricaded myself in the bathroom in my house. I was banging my head against the toilet and cutting my head open with a tiny skeleton key—anything I could possibly do to cause myself harm. I thank God every day that I didn't have my gun with me that day in my bathroom.

As I yelled through the bathroom door, my wife at the time rushed two of our daughters down to the playroom in the basement so they would not witness this extreme behavior. Then she got on the phone to my doctor. "This is Mrs. Weaver. I don't know what to do. Eric's locked himself in the bathroom." She told her to stand by the front door and make sure I didn't run out of the house while she called 911. When this very angry, violent, testosterone-driven, bodybuilding, suicidal SWAT team sergeant found out the police were coming said, "If you bring a rookie deputy into my house, then you better bring about 20 of them because nobody is taking me out of my own home," I screamed. It was the same thing I had heard hundreds of times, answering calls.

Fortunately, a lieutenant I worked for previously in the sheriff's office heard my name on the 911 call and said he would handle the situation alone. Safety wise, it wasn't very smart of him, but he didn't want the other officers to see me in that state. "Eric, this is Lieutenant so and so. You've got to come out," he said knocking on the bathroom door. I didn't care one bit about his rank and answered belligerently, "I don't work for you anymore. The only way I'm coming out of this bathroom is if my Captain orders me out." My wife called my captain, who lived five miles way, and he came down to the house and knocked on the door. "Eric, this is Captain Karnes. Time to come out." I said, "Yes, sir," and was taken to my second hospitalization.

During both hospitalizations, I went to a small hospital in a different county than where I worked. I did not want anyone to know. The hospital was set up for short-term acute care but lacked longer-term treatment for depression and suicidal thoughts, so I was referred to a day treatment program in Rochester, and also advised to attend support groups and see a doctor. I started going to treatment, where I showed up at the hospital every morning, went to counseling and therapy activities, and then went back home again. I did that for about a week or two and then, suicidal thoughts hit really hard again. Once again, I was hospitalized, this time for a couple of weeks in Rochester. I was released, but in just a week or so, I became suicidal again and was hospitalized for a couple more weeks. In short, I was hospitalized five times during the spring, summer, and fall of 1996.

Let me talk a little about what hospitalization was like for me. As a police officer sitting in the emergency room, you know that you're going to be admitted and going someplace that you've taken other people to. I'd taken so many other people to the hospital because of suicide attempts and never really thought much of it. But now, I was the one in the hospital, not knowing what was happening and not really understanding why I was there. Then the door locks behind you and slams shut. They take away your clothes, and suddenly, you feel like you're nobody.

While you're in the hospital, they encourage you to go to a little group with a bunch of other people who are suicidal, depressed, angry, sad, and crying. During most of my stays, the majority of patients were women, which made me feel even more like a failure. What kind of man was I? You stand in line for everything as you're watched 24 hours a day and not allowed to be alone in your room. I knew I needed to be there, but I desperately didn't want to be.

The visiting hours are much different in psychiatric hospitals than regular hospitals. In some of my classes, I ask: "How many people ever been in the hospital? Like you had surgery, you had a baby, whatever? Take your experience in a regular hospital, where you have your own little call button, people bringing you food and flowers, and too many visitors in the room even though they're not supposed to be. Take that experience that you had in a regular hospital, reverse it, and that's what it's like in a psychiatric hospital."

Until my second stay in a psychiatric hospital, no one except my captain and deputy chief knew I was there. But during my third stay, I needed desperately for someone to know where I was. I was so alone and afraid. The loneliness inside of a psychiatric hospital was so intense. All that went through my head was, "No one knows where I am. Only my wife knows where I am. My family kind of knows, but none of the people that I am so close with knows."

So, I asked my wife to reach out to my four closest friends. I was their sergeant, but they were my guys. I trusted these guys with my life. We worked together so closely that I never even thought for a second they would tell anybody else. Cops don't trust anybody. But I did trust them. I trusted them with my life on the street. I was willing to risk them telling somebody just to have them come see me.

One night, they all came in plain clothes. Here I was, walking around with pajama bottoms and no shoes and socks on with my guys. I was their boss, and they were my officers. I remember having a nurse show my four officers a video on depression so they would know why I was there. I needed so desperately for them to know what was happening to their sergeant.

Each time I went into the hospital, I believed it would be my last time. I also knew even when I was released that things were still not right with me. I remember being wheeled out of the hospital during my fourth stay and there sat my wife and kids in our Dodge Caravan. "Daddy's coming home again," she said. I looked up at the nurse as I got into the vehicle and said, "If you allow me to get into this van, this is what I'm going home to do." I then laid out my suicide plan. She re-admitted me about eight minutes after I was just discharged.

In total, I think I spent around two months in and out of hospitals during 1996. My colleagues thought it was for back issues; only my captain, deputy chief, our police physician, and four friends knew what was really going on. And to be honest, the doctors were a bit clueless too about what was going on. I was diagnosed with major depression, but unfortunately it was treatment-resistant which meant that the medication and therapy did not work. Nothing was working. Nothing was helping. Nothing was reducing my suicidal thinking, and at one point they wanted to me to live in a half-way house, which I refused to do.

During my fifth hospitalization, the doctor called my family together and told them that they had run out of options. They didn't know what to do. Their final recommendation was electroconvulsive therapy (ECT). They wanted to essentially jumpstart my brain so the medication could do what it needed to do.

For those of you who do not know, ECT—Electroconvulsive therapy (ECT) is a procedure done under general anesthesia, in which small electric currents are passed through the brain, intentionally triggering a brief seizure. ECT seems to cause changes in brain chemistry that can quickly reverse symptoms of certain mental health conditions. ECT often works when other treatments are unsuccessful and when the full course of treatment is completed, but it may not work for everyone. Much of the stigma attached to ECT is based on early treatments in which high doses of electricity were administered without anesthesia, leading to memory loss, fractured bones and other serious side effects. ECT is much safer today. Although ECT may still cause some side effects, it now uses electric currents given in a controlled setting to achieve the most benefit with the fewest possible risks[1].

When I tell my story, people are always a bit shocked – no pun intended – that I agreed to ECT. Here's my truth: Nothing was working despite a tremendous amount of effort on my part, support from my family and doctors, and a variety of medications. I was feeling utterly hopeless. When my doctor recommended electroconvulsive therapy (ECT), I was in no position to make a lot of decisions for myself. I was just a mess, so as a family we decided to try the procedure even though there is a lot of conflicting thoughts and stigma attached.

For me at that time, ECT was a lifesaver. As I tell people, "All I can say is that I'm still here, and it helped save my life. Yes, it affected parts of my memory – which it does – and it sucked. But I'm alive." The medications I had been taking also began to kick in. Things greatly improved, and my psychiatrist approved me to go back to work.

However, our police department doctor also had to clear me. The first thing I did was obtain a letter from my psychiatrist saying that I could carry my gun. Why was that so important? Decades ago, when someone had mental health issues, they gave him or her a fake gun and would put them on administrative duty, usually at HQ, and were labeled as 'rubber gunners'. It looked like they were really armed, but they were not. I said to myself, "How in the world can SWAT team Sergeant Weaver go to work and not have a gun on? Everybody is going to know something then, right?" So, my psychiatrist wrote the letter saying I was safe, and I went to the police doctor and was open and honest about where I had been. I told him that I was doing really well, and my doctor validated that. My department's doctor and I talked at length, and he signed off that I could return to duty.

By the end of 1996, I was back to work with SWAT as if nothing had changed. As I mentioned, very few people knew the real reason for my absence, so upon returning, I had hundreds of officers asking about my back. It's interesting that most people suffering from mental illness are very convinced that everyone will find out about what they are experiencing. Yes, sometimes that happens. But, more often than not, no one does. In my case, there were 700 people in my department, and only six knew what I had gone through.

Work went really well and in a year, I was hand selected for the Tactical Unit, a very prestigious job in our department. At that point, I did not know what the effect of silence was having on my wellbeing. Today I suspect it was much greater than I knew at the time. But my reason for silence seemed valid. If the stigma of mental illness is still powerful in 2020, imagine what it was like 30 years ago. Then compound it even more with the law enforcement culture.

There was, however, a very high cost for the silence. Two years later, I was back in the worst depression I had experienced. Yet even after all I had been through, I never acknowledged that I had a mental illness. I was Eric Weaver, not one of "those people." I was in denial about having a mental disorder. I was living in a cocoon of silence. And I had to prove to the world—and myself—that I was still an absolute tough guy. I just wasn't some crazy guy locked up in a psych hospital. I had to prove to myself that I was still a man; I was still a sergeant; and I was still somebody. I became angrier, more aggressive, and continued to have affairs almost as much as I did before.

My behavior caught up with me when in 1998, after doing something really stupid, I was brought up on departmental charges and everything was taken from me – may I emphasis deservedly so. I was removed from the SWAT team and tactical unit. I remember crying because I had just gotten a tactical unit tattoo. I was suspended for 15 days and put on administrative duty for one year to get me off the streets. The only thing I was allowed to keep was my sergeant rank.

They put me in the professional development section, because it would be a good place for me to do no damage. I sat there in a cubicle, every day for eight hours with literally nothing to do. Everything that I thought Eric Weaver was made of—SWAT and tactical, street cop and drug intervention—was taken from me. Everything that I put my life into was now gone.

And what was truly remarkable was that even after all of this, I still did not truly acknowledge that I had a mental illness. I chalked it up to just being a bad time, and actually pretended like it never happened – that it was a bad dream. I pretended it went away. I pretended it didn't even exist. And my closest friends who came to see me at the hospital? We never talked about it. They never said, "Sergeant, how are you doing?" Because we just don't talk that way to each other.

One day I found myself in the basement of our old public safety building, quietly telling myself that the time had come. My life as I had known it was over; I could not fight any more. In my hand was my department-issued Beretta 9mm handgun. I was alone and determined that this was how and where I would die. The images of my family passed through my mind briefly—how they would take the news, how the funeral would go, who would be there, and if anyone would even care that I was dead. These images had passed through my mind hundreds of times over the years, but this time was different. Now everyone would learn how much I was hurting inside.

As I slowly started put my finger on the trigger, I heard the sound of water running in the restroom at the end of the locker room. I didn't want anyone around when I killed myself. I wanted to be alone. I quickly put my gun back in my holster, got up, and walked out of the locker room to the restroom, fully expecting to see one of my fellow officers washing his hands.

There was no one at the sink. Was it just my imagination that I heard water running? But now, since no one was there, I was faced with two choices. I could go back and finish what I planned to do, or I could leave. For whatever reason, I chose to leave. Today, I interpret hearing that water as Divine Intervention and grace. Later that day, I admitted myself to the hospital for the sixth time.

After I got back to work after that hospitalization, I had done my six months in the professional development section, doing virtually nothing, and was transferred to another administrative position in the research and evaluation section. This is the section that works on things like general orders and new initiatives. I was now working on the same floor as all the top brass, and fortunately, or unfortunately, I saw all of them each day. Believe it or not, this was a time I used wisely and was able to build a new reputation for myself with my administrators. I worked on numerous projects and was getting accolades from commanding officers that I never thought possible. One day, the chief's secretary looked at me and said, "You know, Eric, you're not as bad as we all thought you were." My immediate thought was, "Oh my gosh! For someone to say that, what did everyone think of me?" Even though it was a very nice thing for her to say, it made quite a bit of impact on knowing how many people perceived me.

So, after my administrative year was up, as promised, Chief Robert Duffy, who was the deputy chief during my hospitalizations and kept it all confidential, put me back in patrol on midnights. I was much more reserved this time around and counted my blessings to even be back doing what I loved. In a story I'll share later, I was assaulted in 1999, and after having surgery as a result, I had enough seniority as a sergeant to be transferred to a day position in a very challenging part of the city. Then something changed.

I had always been a very angry, devout atheist. I didn't believe in anything. A couple of years earlier, I started going to church just to appease my wife. Our pastor was a stately old gentleman who would always visit me in the hospital. He'd stay for 20 minutes talking, and little by little, I started talking to him and began wondering what was going on in my life. Up until that time, even with all the therapy, I had never really been a person of introspection.

Over time, I realized what he was trying to tell me about Jesus and God. In the summer of 2000, I had a moment of intense clarity. "Oh my gosh! So this is who God is. Of course, it all makes sense!" And everything changed. Everything changed. I actually started to become a kind, loving and compassionate person. People started asking, "Sarge, what's happened to you? You don't even swear anymore." I started getting better. I started actually dealing with things. I started working through stuff. I was taking my therapy seriously. By the way, for all of you reading this, please know this is not a book on faith or religion. I know that if it was, half of you would close it and go no further. I know I would have. But I would be totally remiss if I didn't tell you this part of my journey, so please read on.

The other Sergeant Weaver—angry, yelling and swearing, yelling at people—was gone. I think a lot of it had to do with realizing that life wasn't really all about me after all. I realized that there was something out there bigger than me, which I never thought was possible. I realized that there was a God who loved me. It was a wonderful thing to feel—to feel like I was okay.

No, my mental illness didn't go away. It didn't vanish. But I looked at things differently and treated people differently. I was showing empathy for people I never showed empathy before in my life. It wasn't all about Eric Weaver anymore. It all started with breaking the silence.

CHAPTER 4

BREAKING THE SILENCE

In 2002, my life changed dramatically again when a fellow officer killed himself. His name was Eddie Martinez. We worked together as officers, and he worked for me when I was a sergeant. He was a dear friend. When I heard the news, I knew in my heart that God didn't save me from all those suicide attempts and hospitalizations to keep it all to myself. Now the voices in my head that, for decades, had urged me to kill myself were saying something quite different. "Eddie is dead. That should be me. I can't bring him back, but maybe I can do something to prevent it from happening again."

I realized that I needed to share my story with people because other officers were struggling, and even dying. It was time to end the silence. The first thing I did was request to be added to the agenda of the next command staff meeting. They gave me 10 minutes. My intention was not only to tell my story to these captains, deputy chiefs, and commanders, but also to show them that something could be done. Eddie Martinez did not need to take his life.

Standing in front of my superiors, I told them everything that I have relayed so far in this book. For the first time, I came clean about my life between 1996 and 1998. I told them the truth about my mental illness and suicidal thinking. I told them about the hospitalizations. I told them that the back injury story had been a ruse. I told them what silence had cost my family and me. I told them that I no longer wanted to stand by and watch another officer die because I lacked the courage to be honest and transparent about my struggles.

Then I made a request. "Let me put together a presentation about what happened to me. I know that with 700 people in this department, there are lots of problems. Officers are getting divorced, getting into trouble with drugs and alcohol, and now they are killing themselves. Please let me share my story."

The training I proposed would involve talking about the challenges police officers face, and how to prevent suicide and mental illness. This would not be training told in some kind of academic way. This would be training by an officer who had lived the experience; it would be grounded by my own personal account.

The people in the room were shocked when they heard what I had been through. You could see on their faces that they had one big question: "How could we not know what was going on with Eric Weaver?" The answer was simple. My confidentiality had been protected by two men at the meeting – Michael Karnes, my captain, and Bob Duffy, who by then was chief of police, who later went on to become the mayor of Rochester and then Lieutenant Governor of New York State. Both these men respected my confidentiality and privacy very well. They in no way 'covered' for me. But instead, they knew that I was getting help and prevented me being the center of rumors. This is the stand they took: "Eric's got some stuff going on. We're going to help him through those issues. He is going to come out better from it."

I cannot begin to tell you how progressive and compassionate this thinking was in the 1990s and early 2000s. These two men were intent on not jeopardizing my health and career, while at the same time making sure that the department and those we protect were taken care of. I owe my continued career and my very life to God, Captain Karnes, and Chief Duffy, and I have thanked them often over the years. My department was simply amazing at a time when mental illness and trauma were not even talked about.

One captain at the command staff meeting was very skeptical about my desire to break the veil of silence. "Sergeant, this is all well and noble that you want to get up and talk about mental illness and suicide. But you can't get up in front of 700 police officers – especially those that worked with and for you – and tell them that you were in a psychiatric hospital six times."

"Why not?" I asked him directly.

"What would people say, Sergeant?" he curtly replied, staring right at me.

In the past, I might have backed down, feeling shame and guilt. I might have told him he was right and asked everyone in the room to keep my story to themselves. But over the past couple of years, I had been changing profoundly and Eddie's death was a clear sign to me that the silence needed to be broken. In fact, I think of his death as fourth in a series of events that had brought me to stand before these men and women with my request.

The first event was being suspended and then being taken off the SWAT team. At the time, I thought it was the worst thing that ever happened to me. In reality, it was one of the best things that could've happened. I got knocked down quite a few pegs, and it really smacked me upside the head and said, "You got to knock off your shit."

The second event was in the locker room with a gun in my hand. I was seconds away from ending it when I heard the water running in the other room and stopped because I did not want a witness. There was nobody there. I realized that it was Divine

Intervention; the beginning of my understanding that there was something bigger than me calling the shots. At that time, the medication was working. The electro-shock had worked. But what wasn't working was the hard work I needed to do to look at stuff in my life. I had all this medication working for my brain, but nothing was working in my heart.

The third event, when my heart changed a little bit, other stuff started to change too. For me, personally, it was letting Jesus Christ and God into my life. This is a very, very important point. Often people say to me, "Oh! You found Jesus, and it all went away." No, it did not all go away. I was and still am mentally ill, and at times suicidal. As a matter of fact, I've been hospitalized three more times since I retired in 2005: Once in 2008 when I was a pastor, and again as a national trainer/consultant in 2014 and 2017. The latter was at a trauma disorders center in Baltimore. Post-Traumatic Stress Disorder, as well as a few others, are the mental illnesses I live with every day. It is controlled through medication and therapy, but it did not and will not just simply go away. For me, it is a chronic condition that can be debilitating and fatal if not continuously worked on. It means that I have to always be vigilant about my mental health and learn how to deal with things differently. There is no real cure, but recovery is possible. It does not need to take over or end my life.

The fourth event was Eddie's death. Up until then, my primary focus was taking care of my family, my career, and myself. Eddie's death made me realize that I had a higher purpose. I didn't quite know what it was at that point, but I knew my first step was to break the silence in my own department.

So, when I was asked about what people would say, I knew exactly how to respond. "Captain, that's the problem. We're so concerned about what strangers think about us that we're willing to throw away our families, careers, and very own lives. If people don't like Eric Weaver by now, they're not going to. It's not about me. It's about them."

Fortunately for my department, our newly appointed deputy chief of administration at the time was Dr. Cedric Alexander, a clinical psychologist who had done extensive work in the field of officer/employee assistance. He clearly recognized the need for this type of training, and since he oversaw the professional development section of the department, he gave me full permission to teach my class to our entire department.

I titled the class, "Emotional Safety and Survival." This is before I even knew that the very popular book, *Emotional Survival for Law Enforcement* by Kevin M. Gilmartin Ph.D. *(E-S Press 2002),* even existed, otherwise I would have titled it something else. During our department's 2003 in-service training, I taught this 4 hour class every day for six weeks until every one of my 700 fellow officers had gone through it. Officers who had worked with me and for me took it. My commanding officers took it. And I can tell you, those six weeks gave me the chance to see who my real friends were within the department. Some would come to me and say how sorry they were about what I had gone through; others would roll their eyes because they found me stupid and silly. I've now taken this class to more than 30,000 law enforcement officers and emergency services personnel throughout the country.

What I also learned was that my intuition was correct—so many of my fellow officers were in pain from continual post-traumatic and vicarious trauma. At that point, I wasn't even aware of what the impact of trauma really was, but I found out that as soon I started talking about my experiences, the floodgates burst. Officer after officer would call me and ask to meet over coffee and breakfast. They very badly needed to talk; and I think they now felt as though there was someone to talk to.

In 2003, Dr. Alexander, who once again was very ahead of his time in relation to recognizing the need for police mental health training, appointed me project coordinator, and then eventually Commanding Officer of the first Crisis Intervention

Team (CIT) in New York State, which we named, for a variety of reasons, the Emotionally Disturbed Persons Response Team. We had never had such a thing before, but because of my police experience, and yes, my own mental illness and understanding of it, I was chosen to command the CIT (EDPRT) for Rochester. With the encouragement and support of Dr. Alexander, and the Rochester mental health community, we put together the largest police mental health training in the country, a full 80 hours with both basic and advanced courses. My department not only supported the program locally, but also encouraged me to share it with other departments in multiple states.

Imagine me in full police uniform with my badge, medals and a 45 pistol, introducing myself. "Hi, my name is Eric Weaver, a sergeant with the Rochester Police Department and Commanding Officer of the Emotionally Disturbed Persons Response Team, and I'm mentally ill." You should have seen people's faces and bewilderment—what was a cop doing talking about mental illness? I answered their unspoken question. "Well, I know a lot of cops that have heart disease. I know a lot of cops that have diabetes. I know a lot of cops that have ulcers. I'm mentally ill. It's just another illness." Because of his on-going support, I truly owe and thank God and Dr. Alexander for the opportunity to enter my journey into teaching about mental illness.

The doors kept opening, as more departments wanted me to come and talk about mental illness. As I got closer to retirement, I decided to go into ministry after my career as a police officer ended. I wanted to help my church and eventually, I became the executive pastor for five years. I retired in 2005, but my mental illness did not. Even though I was no longer living a life filled with trauma, I did not get an instant cure the day I handed in my badge. In December 2005, when I was scheduled to accept my 20-year certificate at City Hall. All I had to do was walk across the stage, shake Dr. Alexander's (then Chief of Police) hand, and get my long sought after 20-year certificate. I didn't have to give a speech or even say my name. But just before I was called up, for whatever reason, anxiety and stress overwhelmed me. I had my wife tell someone that I got sick and had to leave. As I walked out of City Hall, I asked my wife what was happening to me. I shortly learned thereafter that, because of some obsessive thoughts that I was experiencing as part of my OCD, I had my first panic attack; and I never told anyone.

Over the next five years, I was diagnosed, or misdiagnosed, with a variety of things, from major depression, to bi-polar disorder, to anxiety disorder, etc.. As I mentioned, I ended up hospitalized again – now as a pastor – in 2008. Now imagine me standing in front of a faith community. "My name is Eric Weaver, the executive pastor of the church, and I'm mentally ill." You can imagine what people were thinking. "You're not mentally ill. You're a pastor. You're not supposed to be like that." But no matter if I was a cop or a pastor, I was simply a person with a brain disorder.

As much as I loved the ministry, I felt called to continue my work with law enforcement. I left the ministry in 2010 to create a company that offers training, consulting, and other services to help both law enforcement and community agencies. Our mission is to reduce stigma; increase understanding surrounding the many challenges of mental health related issues; create a culture that openly discusses the topic of mental illness, suicide and suicide related behavior; and above all, proclaim that there is hope.

So here I was doing work that I was absolutely passionate about, but still dealing with mental illness. Finally, in 2013, after working with a wonderful therapist, I was correctly diagnosed with Complex Post-traumatic Stress Disorder (PTSD), and Obsessive-Compulsive Disorder with some psychotic features, as well as one or two more. Much of the PTSD as the result of serving in law enforcement for 22 years; first as a corrections officer, and then as a police officer. As I learned more about PTSD, I found that the depression, anxiety, and even many of the suicidal thoughts were not separate diagnoses but were all indicative of my PTSD and even a bit of my OCD. Even though I was never involved in a police shooting, I spent years seeing things that nobody should see. It caught up to me like it has for so many of my fellow cops. As I mentioned, one of the things that I realized after working with so many officers and departments is that often, the only acceptable trauma we accept is if an officer is involved in a police shooting. We accept that trauma with open arms, yet we take day after day trauma and chalk it up to "Well, that's just our job."

As I continue to work on my own mental health issues, which do include a couple more diagnosis than PTSD, I strive to be a living example that a level of recovery is available to everyone. It is my hope and desire that law enforcement officers and their families will no longer need to suffer in silence, and instead proclaim the fact that the mental illnesses and traumas we are so prone to are treatable, and that suicide is preventable. Today, the law enforcement community struggles with knowing what to do with officers who suffer with mental illness. We are quick to judge and call them unfit for duty. When I talk about mental illness, please know that I talk about it as a professional – from responding to thousands of individuals who are mentally ill, and training officers about how to deal with those who are mentally ill. I also speak from the standpoint of living with mental illness and suicide every day. With that context, I invite you to move on to the next chapter as we look at the particular stressors that are part of the police culture.

CHAPTER 5

STRESSORS AND THE POLICE CULTURE

I was out near Wichita, Kansas doing police training when a young officer who had only been on the job six months said to me, "Hey Sarge, you've been retired now for 10 years and the job sure has changed since you've been on it, right?" I smiled at him. "You know, you might have fancy computers in your cars and can print out a ticket on a printer instead of an old carbon-copy, but I absolutely guarantee that the conversations you have in your locker room are exactly the same conversations I had in mine."

I've shared that conversation over the last few years in my classes, and literally every officer in the room nods his or her head in agreement. Not much has changed in certain aspects of police culture since I joined in 1983 at age 20 – almost 40 years ago. Yes, the challenges have changed with new laws, technology and social media. But the personal, professional, and emotional challenges? Not so much. I'm talking about the way we talk about and to each other as well as the fact that we are not very good at taking care of ourselves. And we have things relating to police culture that we simply will not discuss. If things had really changed and we were having honest discussions, the rates of suicide, domestic violence, divorce, substance use, and more wouldn't be so high. But it is not hopeless. I truly believe that we can help ourselves reduce those rates by openly addressing some of the obvious and unique problems our culture creates.

For example, I have discussed the stigmas that society, and law enforcement officers specifically, have about getting critical help when faced with mental health issues. Too often, even asking for help is looked at as a sign of weakness. While our society in general is trying to get better at supporting people in need, still only half of people in the U.S. dealing with mental illness seek help[1]. I'm pretty certain that among law enforcement, that percentage is much, much lower.

So, what is it about the police culture that prevents us from getting the help we need? One huge factor is how we deal with emotions. Law enforcement officers are conditioned to not show emotion in situations and circumstances where the average person would react with horror, fear, and disgust. It's not that we actually go to the academy and take Don't Show Emotion 101. It's simply that we get conditioned to not show how we are feeling—"You know, it's just a dead baby. What am I going to get upset for?" After years of this, we can easily start shutting down all emotion—not only with each other, but also with our families. Please don't think I am painting all law enforcement with the same brush. I know many officers do discuss emotions, and that critical incident debriefings take place. But both of those things are more the exception than the rule.

In his book, *Police Passages*[2], Dr. John G. Stratton discusses numerous issues that are specific to the law enforcement culture and that many other occupations don't necessarily have to deal with. Some of these stressors are internal, caused by the work itself. Others are personal and affect us individually and as a culture. What I do know is that the stressors he discusses exist as strongly today as they did in 1984, when he wrote his book – one year after I joined the force. Most of the bolded points are his, with my explanation, and I've added a few of my own in order to discuss other law enforcement cultural issues.

Poor/Inadequate Training

Training among officers varies widely among individual departments based on their budgets, priorities, and desire for enhanced training. Training usually is based on any given department's priorities. If departments believe a certain issue is important, they'll provide training. If they don't, they will not, unless it is mandated. Some departments offer training for their officers on a regular basis, while others do not. Take the training I now do for officers dealing with issues of mental health—specifically how to respond to an individual in a mental health crisis. Departments vary from providing 40 hours of Crisis Intervention Team (CIT) training and other mental health training, to only incorporating a few hours as part in their academy. Obviously, with knowledge comes understanding and the ability to make better decisions for not only the citizens that officers protect, but also for themselves. That's why I believe strongly that ongoing training in law enforcement requires the same commitment as other professions like teachers and doctors.

In recent days, the concept of defunding the police and reducing budgets is a scary one. When police department's budgets become cut, one of the very first things to go is training, because of the cost of funding the officers to attend and paying overtime to cover the shifts of those who are out training. Training is the exact thing that communities are asking us to have more of, but unfortunately, you can't have both without one impacting the other.

Poor Supervision

We've all experienced great bosses and not so great bosses. A good supervisor relieves many of the stressors faced by officers by the way he or she handles internal problems, scene management, and overall performance. A poor supervisor can create and add to the havoc, stress, and negative environment on a job that already has havoc, stress, and a negative environment. A good supervisor has the exact opposite effect. That's why on-going supervisor training and evaluation is a critical part of any well-functioning agency.

A good supervisor builds you up and equips you to be better. A poor supervisor tears you down and berates you for not being good enough. A good supervisor can make you actually look forward to going to work. A poor supervisor has officers taking as many days off as possible or calling in sick, just because they know a specific supervisor is working that day. A good supervisor treats everyone equally. A poor supervisor favors some of his or her officers and ignores and ostracizes others. This applies to the Chief or Sheriff, and right down to the midnight sergeant. If you're a supervisor reading this, you probably know if you are a good or poor supervisor. If you're not sure, ask your officers.

Poor Career Development Opportunities

Career opportunities vary based upon the size of the department. Some departments are big enough that there is potential for movement—from one section to another, from Vice to K-9, or from one shift to another. I was fortunate to be in a department of more than 700 officers, where there were many opportunities. It might have taken a bit of time to get off midnight shifts and go to days, go from one section to another, or to be involved in a specialized team, but the opportunity was there.

The majority of departments that are smaller – and there are many across the country—have little opportunity for career growth and development. Many officers realize that they will be stuck on a shift for years, with no chance of changing, until a fellow officer retires. They know that there are only a handful of sergeant or investigator positions available. They know that they can't go anywhere. I have found this to be a major stressor for many officers over the years. Obviously, there is not much that can be done to change the size of a department, but in some smaller departments, officer morale is high and stress is low. In others, it is the opposite. Learning from those small departments that are doing it right can help alleviate this stress factor.

Offensive Department Policies

From having to wear your hat every time you exit your vehicle, to allowing no more than two cars at a restaurant at any given time, department polices can create tremendous stress for officers. One reason is that a violation of any specific sub-section of what looks like a random policy can result in disciplinary action. Even more importantly, often officers feel that some policies make their job more difficult, tie their hands, and don't allow them to do their job effectively.

This is an area that police officers are stuck with unless they have the ability and authority to change policies. However, leadership that creates, evaluates and changes policies that reflect the best interests of the officers, as well as the community and department, goes a long way in creating a culture with less stress.

Excessive Paperwork

Many occupations such as health care providers require significant documentation. It's no different for law enforcement, except that the level of outside scrutiny from the public and in court is even more intense. Every written word and the smallest of errors are under review. From department crime reports, investigative summary forms, prisoner data sheets, state forms, property sheets, lab request forms, medical screenings, booking forms, use of force reports, mental hygiene/hospital forms, juvenile packages, DWI tickets, observation forms, search warrants and countless others, excessive and repetitive paperwork can be absolutely overwhelming.

Some documentation is the result of department policies while local, state, and federal laws require others. Whatever the case, the amount of paperwork, now mostly done via computer programs, is not going to change and will probably grow. How can police agencies help officers with this stressful and important part of their jobs, particularly as the number of incidents they are responding to also continues to grow? Modern technology can help speed up the process, but the major stressor of the overabundance of detailed documentation still looms.

Role Conflict: Services vs. Enforcement

The majority of law enforcement officers were asked in their initial interview, "Why do you want this job?" Most responded that it was because they wanted to help people. But over the years, whether in policing or corrections, we become either the typical crime fighter or lean towards the social service side of our work. Many officers tend to focus on one versus the other because it is easier. These dual aspects of the job can be a difficult stressor in our culture. Either I arrest someone every chance I get, or I embrace a community-policing model where we focus on police and community relationships. This same duality exists in corrections work. Do I treat everyone as just another inmate, or do I encourage inmates to get involved in education, support groups, and other programs? Is it possible to find a happy medium? The answer is yes, but it is harder. Not doing so, however, creates real stress. Again, more training, clearer career paths and supportive supervision can help resolve this role conflict.

Shiftwork

Midnights, afternoons, weekends, and holidays? Imagine what that does to your life. While many departments have better scheduling options than in the past such 10-hour days, every other weekend off, or three days off in a row, many retain a more traditional model that has officers working one month of days, one month of afternoons, and one month of midnights on a rotating basis. In some smaller departments that don't have a lot of turnover, officers know that they will be stuck on midnights or afternoons for years. These types of schedules can make it very difficult, not only for the officers, but also for their families.

When I was on the job, our department had a schedule of four days on and two days off. This 4-2, 4-2, 5-2 schedule meant that we would have an actual Saturday and Sunday off, about every two months or so. I also worked midnights for a number of years, and to be honest, it was horrible. I remember darkening out my windows with black cardboard, taking Benadryl to try to sleep, and pretty much everything else I could think of. But then you wake up from your neighbor mowing the lawn, the kids running around the house despite your wife or husband telling them to be quiet, or the district attorney's office calling at noon to tell you that you're needed in court in two hours. Afternoons have issues also. It's usually not too bad for those officers who are single, but it can wreak havoc on a family.

Lack of sleep from scheduling can result in memory problems, reduced cognition, decreased alertness, and a whole host of medical problems.[3] Add this to missing important family activities like your kid's soccer game, and you create stress both personally and professionally. Progressive departments can help solve scheduling issues to a large extent by experimenting with different ways to maintain coverage while reducing stress on their officers.

Fear and Danger

This stressor, which is a given for law enforcement, is pretty much self-explanatory. No matter who you are, there are situations that can cause tremendous fear. I could certainly give hundreds of examples, but those in law enforcement and corrections understand that even though we may not show it, some circumstances can be very frightening. Fear can be both lifesaving and life threatening and is driven by the concept of fight/flight/freeze.

Although all three are reactions by all human beings, freeze is not an option for law enforcement officers. We must act, not freeze. We actually do have the flight option – something we call a tactical retreat, which sounds better than flight. Yet, even when retreat happens, we regroup and go back. In practice, tactical retreat is a rarity. I may have called a tactical retreat once in my 13 years as a supervisor. It was when a few officers were getting rocks and bottles thrown at them at a house party on a dead-end street. I got all of us out, but then we went back in force and shut it down.

For law enforcement officers in danger, the overwhelming option is fight, and danger is often present. We end up being hyper vigilant. Constantly on alert and perceiving the world as a place where danger is all around can cause extreme stress in officers. Whether you're responding to a call of shots fired or a fight in a cell block, we know that danger is always present. We have had officers shot and killed while just sitting in their cars, and correction officers assaulted and killed in the recreation yard. This day after day after day work environment can be very taxing, leading to stress and causing both emotional and physical repercussions.

There is no way to take fear and danger out of law enforcement. But how we process and react to it has options. I'm not saying that we sit in a sharing circle every day and talk about our fears. However, breaking the code of silence and acknowledging the daily stress – not just major incident stress – can go a long way in helping reduce emotional and physical problems.

Absence of Closure

I shared the story of the kid who hung himself in the jail, and my need to see him alive. I needed closure. Often, however, law enforcement officers have no idea about what happens to the people they come in contact with. I spent a lot of time, for example, on child abuse cases and submitted countless Department of Social Services or Child Protective referrals. At the bottom of the referral form, it asks, "Do you want to be contacted as a result of this investigation?" I always checked, 'Yes' but never got a phone call in my whole career. This is also true about arrests. Contrary to television shows, police officers don't go to court all that often. Cases get pled out, dismissed, or referred somewhere else.

So quite often we never know whatever happened to the people that we dealt with. This continued absence of closure during an officer's career can be a very difficult stressor. Like the fear and danger stressor, there is no way around it but how we acknowledge, and process can help.

People Pain

Law enforcement officers see people on the worst days of their lives—death, child abuse, rape, overdoses, and suicides. The list is endless. We see people during their darkest hour day after day, after day, after day. After a while, this pain affects us whether we want it to or not. If it doesn't affect you even a little, then you need to tell us the secret and write your own book. Or perhaps, check your pulse.

Responsibility for Other People's Safety

Even though we talk about officer safety, the reality is that we're primarily responsible for the safety of other people. From an active shooter situation to guarding someone on suicide watch, other people's lives are in our hands. Imagine the enormous stress when you have a shooter across from a kindergarten that you've been tasked to evacuate. Or how you feel pulling someone from a burning car. Even after taking someone into custody, we are responsible for his or her safety and wellbeing. Whether in a day room or walking through the cell block, we're responsible for the safety and wellbeing of the inmates.

This responsibility doesn't get acknowledged much in police culture. We don't talk about the fact that other people's lives are in our hands. But year after year of this kind of daily stress can greatly affect our lives, both personally and professionally. And once again, the solution is to break the silence.

Consequences of One's Actions

If you are in law enforcement, you are responsible for everything you do, write or say. In today's world, your actions and, in some cases, lack of action, easily end up on YouTube in a matter of minutes. This is unlike any other profession. With body cameras recording every move we make and every word we speak, the stress can be profound.

Knowing the consequences of our actions can actually be threatening to our lives and affect officer safety. In 1991, I got a call for a loud music complaint. It was a Monday morning around 8 a.m. and getting a loud music complaint at that time of day was kind of unusual. I was annoyed. I was a field-training officer at the time, and it was literally my recruit's first day. The complaint interrupted my coffee time, and I was saddled with a recruit, which meant I couldn't blow off the complaint.

The apartment was on the fourth floor, and when we got there, blaring music was coming from inside. I banged on the door and someone said, "Who is it?" I replied, "It's the police." "Who?" Once again, I said, "The police." Again, the response was, "Who?" I yelled, "The police" as I heard footsteps shuffling and sounds of a toilet flushing. Who knew what they were trying to get rid of? I was already annoyed to be there, so now I was even more annoyed that they didn't answer the door. When a guy finally opened the door and stood behind it, my officer safety training went out the window. I stepped into the open doorway just like we're trained never to do.

There was a guy about eight feet away sitting on a couch with a loaded .45 pointed at my head. Keep in mind as I share this that I was a SWAT sniper at this point in my career. I understood deadly physical force very well. I stepped back, took cover behind the doorframe, and drew my 9mm. "Drop the gun. Drop the gun," I screamed numerous times. At that point in my life, I did not have suicidal ideations, so I wasn't looking for a way out. I also had a recruit with me on his first call ever, and was responsible for him as well.

It seemed like forever that I was telling him to drop the gun as my sights focused on his head. Yet as I yelled, part of my brain screamed to shoot him while another part of my brain was loudly saying things such as, "You know you're going to grand jury. You know they're going to take your gun away. You know you're going to have to go to internal affairs. You know your kids are going to hear about this." Those thoughts were what we called back in the day, "nuisance thoughts"—intrusive thoughts that sometimes get in an officer's way, when acting upon a threat during a deadly physical force situation.

This went on for at least 15 seconds before he lowered the gun, switched hands, and came back up with it. Now, part of my brain was screaming even louder to shoot him. The other half was saying just as loud, "You know what's going to happen." After another five seconds of us pointing guns at each other, he tossed his out of an open window behind him and arrogantly crossed his arms. As I handcuffed him and the other guy, I told my recruit to clear the rest of the apartment. What I realized was that I could have easily lost both my life and that of the recruit because of the intrusive thoughts about the consequences of my actions – those nuisance thoughts. That's truly how much of a stressor those thoughts of consequences can be. Situations like this happen every day, except you'll never see them on the 6 p.m. news.

By the way, talk about absence of closure, I have no idea what happened to the people we arrested. The gun was stolen from a burglary, so we charged him with criminal possession of a weapon and possession of stolen property. We also charged him with menacing and everything else that we could. I have no idea what happened to the man who could have killed me. I never went to court or even a preliminary hearing.

Recently, I was sitting in my counselor's office when I started to drift off and disconnect from our conversation—a symptom of PTSD. Out of the blue, I asked my counselor why I didn't shoot that guy in 1991 – 27 years later. Was I glad that I didn't shoot? Very glad. Would I have made a different choice today? Who knows? But 27 years later, the consequences of my actions, and in-actions, were still on my mind.

Incompetence

Incompetence doesn't mean you don't know what you're doing. Incompetence means you might be put in a position you've never been in before. You simply just don't know what to do. That doesn't make you a bad cop or correction's officer. Despite what we say, none of us have "seen it all." There's always something we've never experienced.

When I first got promoted to a sergeant in 1992, I didn't go to supervisor school for about six months after I got promoted.

My promotion meant that one day I was wearing a silver badge, and the next day I was wearing a gold badge. During my first two weeks of being a sergeant, my lieutenant was off on vacation. I was on my own during two very busy weeks filled with shootings and stabbings. I really didn't know what to do as a supervisor. I knew what my role was as an officer, but this was obviously different. I wasn't a bad supervisor, but I just didn't know what I was doing. I was simply put into a position that I had never experienced before.

Many officers can relate to how it felt that first few weeks out of the academy. You might have been the top recruit in the academy, and then you go to field training and are overwhelmed and lost. The feelings of incompetence, whether for someone brand new or even for the most experienced officer, can easily become a major stressor. And here's where police culture comes in. You can't admit to feeling overwhelmed and lost, because you will be seen as weak. So, to appear strong, you fake it until you make it. Imagine the stress of struggling with a new job and not really being able to talk honestly about it. We need to foster a culture that lets people admit when they are feeling over their head without consequences to their career.

Poor Physical Condition

Working midnights, eating fast food, excessive stress, and lack of proper sleep are all contributors to poor physical condition – a state detrimental for any officer to do his or her job effectively. Here is the irony—There are incredibly few departments that require their officers to maintain a level of physical fitness once they are on the job. Prior to being accepted and while they are in the academy, they must be physically fit. After graduation, however, there are usually no standards. While there are departments that offer incentives or free gym memberships, rarely do they mandate a level of fitness. This is a contributing factor to why those in law enforcement have such a higher level of heart disease than many other occupations[4]. How do you change the police culture about this vital aspect of self-care? Quite simply, all we can do is teach the importance of physical fitness.

Non-Conformity

This is such an absolutely important issue in our current police culture. Non-conformity boils down to this – and female officers understand this as well as men—you're either one of the boys or you're not. If you're one of the boys, life isn't going to be so bad. If you're one of the boys, your career is not so bad. You have people to hang out with, talk to during roll call, consistently back you up, have a couple of beers with, invite you over for a barbecue, and connect with while on the job and at home. If you're not one of the boys, your career is going to be very long. So, what's an impressionable young officer to do? All of a sudden you realize that it's easier to be one of the boys. You start doing things that maybe you wouldn't have normally done if you weren't a cop. You start swearing more, acting more aggressive towards people, and using inappropriate humor—just to fit in.

I know this stressor very well. I never swore or drank until I started working in the jail. After becoming a cop, I acted and behaved for many years in ways I would have never dreamed of. What I eventually learned—which I wish I had learned a long time ago—is something we often teach our children. Pick your friends very wisely. Your friends in policing will make or break your career.

Minority Employees: Ethnic and Female

You wouldn't know it by my last name, but I'm half Puerto Rican. With a last name like Weaver, I could pretty much hide that I was a minority throughout my career, especially since everyone thought I looked Italian. Even so, fellow officers have called me "spic" and "wetback" countless times. The truth is that policing is a very male white-dominated profession.[5] That's how

54

it's always been, and probably always will be. What that means is that minority officers often have entirely different stressors and levels of stress from their male white counterparts, because they are considered to be outside the norm.

Female officers sometimes have it even worse. I am embarrassed by how I used to think of female officers assigned to my shift. "We got a girl with us now? Oh my gosh." I was never quite sure how good she was going to be. She needed to prove herself. "Let's see how she is in a fight, then we'll know whether or not she's good enough to be with us." If she wrote good reports, I would make sure she did the majority of them. I was not unusual among supervisors or officers and am not at all proud of my behavior, but unfortunately, it still remains a real part of our culture.

Sgt. Kiersten Harzewski of the New Mexico State Police, a 26-year veteran female officer, adds this perspective about working in a male dominated profession:

I began my career in law enforcement in 1994, working for a city police department in New Mexico, and about five years into it, my marriage ended. My husband at the time was also in law enforcement and had been for five years before I began my career, which, I have to say, he did not approve of. When I said that I was going to join law enforcement with him, it caused stress in the marriage. He went to the extent of trying to get the organization not to hire me by speaking to those in charge.

Throughout my 26-year career, I've often doubted my chosen profession, wondering how different my life would have been had I stayed working as a paralegal at a law firm. Husbands just couldn't deal with the stigma of having a wife that was in law enforcement. Problems arose from having to work with men all the time. Being able to work through problems in the field and taking control of situations daily does not leave you to be a wife that needs a lot of help. Confidence, strength, independence, and law

*enforcement credentials are not the most feminine quali-
ties. I like to think that learning more about the effects of
the trauma on the job, and understanding the culture and
myself within that culture, has made a difference. I no
longer feel I have something to prove to the officers I work
with. I'm at peace with my own skills and abilities. I've
learned that balancing my skills as a wife, mother, and
police officer has made me happy, fulfilled, and resilient.
I couldn't imagine having chosen another career. My life
of service at home and at work now makes sense to me.*

*I get asked questions by the organization I work for about
hiring and retaining women in law enforcement. In an
organization of approximately 600 officers, 35 are female. My response is that it takes a bigger perspective.
Think not just about hiring women, but about changing
the culture of law enforcement and considering the role
of women globally. Instead of asking the question, "How
do we hire more women in law enforcement," we need to
be asking, "How can we show that law enforcement is a
woman's profession?" It is no longer a career for strong
men who can muscle their way through. It's a career for
people who can think, adapt, solve problems, fix problems
with de-escalation skills, work outside of an ego in order
to come up with a solution that works for everyone, and
above all, realize that this is a life of service. And yes, in
rare occasions, use force to serve and protect. Sounds like
the perfect role of a woman, a mother, a wife.*

Marv Patterson, with 32 years of experience as a police officer and investigator, gives his perspective on his experience as a
black police officer in a mainly male white profession:

*As a black police officer, I can attest to wanting to "fit in"
while the majority of the police departments in the area
were predominately made up of white police officers. My experiences around the predominately white population were*

different. I had recently served on active duty with the US Army, was raised in a suburban neighborhood, and went to public and private schools that were predominately white. I was used to being the "minority" amongst the majority.

My parents brought us up in a Christian home, and we were taught not to discriminate against anyone, even though others may have been prejudiced against us because we were black. My father grew up in South Carolina, and served in the US Army during the 50's-60's, when racial tensions were very high. His accounts regarding racism were very real, and I never experienced discrimination to that degree. Sure, when I was young, I was called racial slurs, but it didn't nearly amount to what my father went through, or several of my relatives who served in predominately white organizations.

Even though I didn't experience "in your face" discrimination on the police department due to color, I eventually realized it came in "different forms." As a male black police officer, I could handle myself physically, and I trained in the martial arts since I was younger. When I attempted to join special units or teams either in the US Army or the police departments, I felt like I had to "double" prove myself against my white counterparts in order to be included on any team. I constantly had to score higher on tests and in events, run faster and show a higher proficiency in tactics, just to prove I was worthy of a special assignment.

The solution? To continue to create and accept a culture that remains to be inclusive of all who wear the uniform, and where no one is above or below anyone else.

Poor coping mechanisms

I've heard it a thousand times, and I've said it a thousand times—We might have bad days, but we think we know how to deal with it. We laugh it off and move on. We get drunk and laugh and do it all again tomorrow. If we have a problem with our wives, there is always the waitress down the street. We 'self-medicate' to try to escape the reality of our stress and trauma in a variety of ways—sex, pornography alcohol, food, prescription and non-prescription drug abuse, gambling, or shopping. We self-medicate so we can feel—even for an hour—outside ourselves and outside our reality. Unfortunately, no matter how hard we try, we find that it never quite satisfies us, so we keep on doing that behavior in hopes that it will somehow miraculously change our lives.

As I have mentioned, cop humor and telling war stories are a big part of police culture. We believe we use these coping mechanisms to relieve stress. The problem is that they don't work. If they worked, we would not see the high suicide, alcoholism, and domestic violence rates among law enforcement. As I previously mentioned, if just telling war stories and talking about our trauma to each other worked, my classes would be four minutes long. It just doesn't work. It's killing us. That's what we need to change.

Bullying

Bullying doesn't just happen in the schoolyard. It happens in colleges, offices, and in nursing homes. It also happens in law enforcement. We are often not very kind to one another; we find each other's weaknesses and pounce. We pick on and ridicule each other. We berate and criticize each other. This is an unfortunate reality, and if you have any kind of sensitive nature to criticism, or heaven forbid you're not one of the boys, you can fall victim to what culture considers simply good old-fashioned kidding or humor. In looking up synonyms for bullying, you'll find harassment, discrimination, and intimidation. Do those happen in law enforcement? I've had officers tear up when I talk about this aspect of our culture. Remember my story of being hit for not splashing somebody as I drove around a puddle? Funny to him. Bullying to me. That's not the media or society doing that to us. That's us doing that to ourselves. Only we can stop it by changing our behavior.

Promoting mental health stigmas

Remember that age-old advice from your mom, grandma, or Aunt Marge—If you don't have something nice to say, don't say anything? As I have mentioned, the conversations in my locker room before I retired are still pretty much the same ones that are going on now. Here's an example of what I mean: Three officers are in a locker room changing before their shift. Officer Jones speaking to Officer Smith, "Hey, did you hear about Joe? Heard he was talking to the Sarge about him being stressed out over work and his divorce. Are you kidding me? Now they're giving him some time off. That's a bunch of bullshit! I got stress too, but you don't hear me whine and complain about it. Now we're running short staffed and being forced to work overtime just because his lazy ass is stressed out and he can't handle everyday life. What a loser. All right, man, talk with you later."

Sound familiar? Every time I ask that question in my seminars, the answer is yes. So, here's my point. What did Officer Jones do to his fellow officer, Joe? He ridiculed him behind his back, made light of whatever he's going through, dismissed him as being lazy, and blamed him for having to work overtime. He mocked him in front of another officer and may or may not have been even accurate as to why Joe needed time off.

But even worse than that, what did Officer Jones do to Officer Smith? First, he certainly reinforced that if he ever had a problem, he knows who not to go to. Plus—and this a very important point—what if that was the very day that Officer Smith's wife told him, "You know, honey, how much me and the kids love you. We don't want to lose you. We're going through some tough stuff, and last night you promised me you would make that phone call to EAP today, remember? I love you."

After running into Officer Jones in the locker room, what do you think that chances are of Officer Smith making that phone call to EAP (Employee Assistance Program) that day? Pretty slim to none. The very human response would be, "I don't want anyone to talk about me that way." And when he gets home and his wife asks him if he made that call, what do you think he'll say? Probably something like, "Sorry honey, busy day...didn't have a chance. Maybe later this week." Which, as we know, means, "I'm not going to call." I'll take it a step further. What if on the other side of the locker room where no one could see him was Officer Peters? He heard the whole tirade of Officer Jones talking to Officer Smith, and that day his wife made him promise to make a phone call to EAP. Once again, what do you think was Officer Peters' chance of making that phone call? Slim to none, for the exact same reason.

In police culture, we call each other brothers and sisters in blue. We say that we are there for each other and that we have each other's backs. But the above conversation takes place in police locker rooms, roll call rooms, talking side by side, car to car, and in many other situations where officers find themselves talking about one another. Once again, that's not the media doing that to us. That's not the bad guys or society doing that to us. That's not our administration or city/county governments doing that to us. It's us doing it to ourselves. Then we wonder why cops don't get help. The fear of what others will say is a very real thing, and it has barely changed an iota over the decades. It starts with leadership and examples. It starts with the individual. It starts with not tolerating this behavior.

The belief that we shouldn't 'tell' on each other

This is really not what you're thinking, and in a way goes with the above section on promoting stigma. As I'll mention in the suicide section, if someone is at risk of suicide and refuses your help, tell someone else. People generally understand the importance of that. However, when I say, "Tell someone else," outside of the suicide issue, officers immediately think of the word 'rat' or 'snitch,' something no officer wants to be labeled as. But when I speak of 'telling someone else,' I'm speaking of the many mental health/addiction issues we see in our profession. 'Telling someone else' can also be called *early intervention*. Here's an example conversation:

"Hey Steve, can I talk with you about something?"

"Sure."

"Well, you're good friends with Keith, right? Well, I've been noticing that he's been acting really off lately."

"What do you mean?"

"The other night we all went out, and he got so drunk that someone had to take him home, and this isn't the first time. I know he's got a wife and two little kids at home, but he's been seeing this waitress on the side. I was going to go talk with him to see if he is ok, but I don't know him that well, and I know the two of you are really good friends, and he seems like he's going downhill really fast. So, I thought that maybe if you talked with him, maybe he'll be able to tell you about what's going on."

Is that being a rat or a snitch? Or is that truly looking out for and caring for one another? Many of us see a fellow officer get divorced, and we say, "Well, we all knew that was coming." My thought is that if you 'knew that was coming,' did anyone ever approach him and say, "Hey, man...What's going on? I don't know if you know what people are seeing but......"

Many of us are in each other's business all the time, but then we see something happen and we say, "Hey, none of my business." We can't really have it both ways. We talk *about* each other a lot. However, we don't talk *with* one another nearly as much as we should. Letting someone else know how another officer is struggling isn't being a rat or a snitch. It's called being a friend.

Hollywood/Television

Starsky and Hutch. CSI Miami. Barney Miller. Super Troopers. Lethal Weapon. Robocop. Training Day. Law enforcement is the most portrayed, albeit misrepresented, profession in the world with depictions anywhere from comical bumbling idiots to unfeeling robots to drug dealing menaces. The role of police in Hollywood and television is in fact purely entertainment, where police solve horrific crimes in two hours or shoot 10 people without thinking twice. They are either viewed as heroes or villains, again, purely for entertainment. But in real life behind the uniform and riot gear are real people; Men and women who have dedicated their lives to serving others. Unfortunately, many of the world's perceptions of policing are based on what they see in movies and TV. That creates a completely distorted view of reality that a large portion of society does not understand.

Media

The media, including social media, can be an incredibly useful tool for police. It can do anything from warning communities of escaped prisoners, to helping locate missing children. It can show police officers delivering toys, having country-wide department sing offs, taking pictures with kids, saving people from burning cars, and playing basketball with members of the community. However, a person doesn't have to look very far to see and hear that the media can also be very unfriendly and rather detrimental to law enforcement in general. Never before has an officer's actions been able to be instantaneously posted on the Internet, quickly picked up and broadcasted by both local and national news within minutes, and then shown over and over again around the world. While in my day there were video cameras, in today's world of technology and smart phones, this has never been more of a stressor. Social media, along with modern-day body cameras can keep officers accountable, which is ultimately not a bad thing, and can actually be used to exonerate officers from false allegation against them.

But at the same time, it creates stress that no other occupation in this country must deal with on a daily basis. For instance, the next time you or one of your family members has to have surgery, ask the doctor if you can be in the room recording it while the surgery is being done. They will say 'No' for a variety of reasons, one of which is in the event of malpractice, it would all be on video. Instead of hiding cameras in a child's backpack, ask teachers to wear body cameras so we know what they really say to our kids and what they really talk about in the teacher's lounge. It will never happen. I could easily give more examples, but I think my point is clear. Like I mentioned, no other occupation has this same type of constant daily stress of being continually recorded.

Civil Unrest

As I write this, our country is experiencing tremendous civil unrest in regard to the horrific incident that took place in Minneapolis, Minnesota on May 25th, 2020. No city, department, and officer want terrible tragedies like this to occur. But when they do, departments all around the country pay the price for the actions of an officer working 3,000 miles away, as we in Rochester experienced during the Los Angeles riots in 1991 and many times since. Sometimes civil unrests last for a couple of days or like this current situation, it can last for weeks. This takes a tremendous toll, both physically and mentally, on a department and on individual officers. Officers are working extra-long days without a day off, being screamed at, assaulted, and disparaged by the community they serve.

As you can imagine, we know that this also takes a tremendous toll on an officer's family as well. A fellow officer in a large department in the south told me that during this current civil unrest, he had not seen his 11 year old son in nearly three weeks, and when he did, the first words out of his mouth were, "Daddy, did anyone shoot at you or throw rocks at you today?" There is no other occupation in the United States in which a child asks that question to a parent. This, along with the long hours, emotional and physical fatigue, cumulative stress, and trauma these events cause, are not doing us any favors. Is it a stressor we have to live with? Sadly, yes. But how we cope and live with it makes all the difference as we will discuss throughout this book.

Retirement

You may be reading this and saying to yourself, "Retirement? How in the world could that be stressor? I can't wait!" But believe it or not, it can be a huge one. When I retired in 2005, I had literally spent more years of my life in law enforcement than I hadn't. The day I turned in my badge was one of the most bittersweet moments of my life. One minute I felt like I was somebody, and the next minute I felt like I was a nobody. I know many law enforcement officers that stay on the job for 25, 30, 35 years because sometimes in reality, that's all they know. That's where their friends are, that's who their families are familiar with, and that's where for many, find their identity. For many officers, retirement is an incredibly joyous feeling, where they are now free to do something else they've always wanted to do. However, for others, once an officer retires and leaves his or her law enforcement family, they feel alone and disassociated from the culture they were once a part of, and isolation and depression can easily take hold.

I remember going to police union dinners and special events, and there were always countless officers that had retired a decade or more still showing up to each event because that's where their family was. During this time of civil unrest, an officer in Rochester was assaulted by a group of individuals, and it happened in my old car beat when I was just an officer. My desire to jump back into uniform and go help was strong. But my feeling of being completely helpless was even stronger. Military veterans can experience the same thing. Once done with a tour overseas, there is often a sense of guilt that they have left their fellow soldiers behind, and that they should be back and be with them. Hence one of the reasons military members go back on deployment is to be with their fellow soldiers.

For all of you reading this who is either in law enforcement or has a family member or loved one in law enforcement, retirement can be a very difficult time. For some, it can be a time of great joy. For others, however, it can be a time of loneliness, despair, and depression. Families and friends need to be very aware of this harsh reality.

Conclusion

I've talked about many aspects of police culture, and there are probably some I have missed. We've focused in on those parts of police culture that add stress to being in law enforcement. Some things we can't do a lot about, like the media and public scrutiny, but much of what I discussed we can do something about, especially when it comes to how we treat one another. We can do better than how we have been.

CHAPTER 6

DEBUNKING THE STIGMA OF MENTAL ILLNESS

I am standing in front of a room of police officers. The topic is mental health, and I can see from their body language that they would prefer to be in many other places instead of this training class. Mental health is not an easy topic for them, or anyone else for that matter. I start by throwing out a statistic from the 2018 National Survey on Drug Use and Health. One out of five Americans experience mental illness in any given year[1]. It's a widely accepted statistic by the mental health community, but it can be startling to people not in the field.

I discuss what that means in real terms; One out of five mail carriers. One out of five Wal-Mart workers. One out of five high school teachers. And one out of five law enforcement officers. Later, I will share my view that the number of law enforcement officers is higher because of the cumulative stress and trauma that those in law enforcement experience, but for now I just want to focus on the impact that one out of five officers has a mental illness. So, I have them counting off by fives. "One, two, three, four, five. You've got it! One, two, three, four, five. You've got it too."

People always laugh when I do this, whether I'm speaking to police officers or medical professionals. They look around the room, point at their friends, their bosses, or fellow co-workers, and informally diagnose them with some form of mental illness. The laughter during this exercise lasts for about a minute. Then, after the crowd calms down, I ask this: "What if I said that one out of five people in this room will be diagnosed with cancer in the next year?"

I then start counting off by fives again, but this time the room is incredibly quiet. There is no laughter or finger pointing, just sullen faces hoping I won't point to them. "Why is no one laughing?" I ask. The answer seems obvious, doesn't it? Cancer is not funny. I know firsthand that mental illness is not funny either. So what is all that laughter called when I counted off by fives regarding mental illness? It's called stigma.

We all understand that mental health, just like physical health, plays an important role at every stage of our lives. But what comes to mind first when you hear the words "mental health" or "mental illness?" For most of us, our first response might be; depressed, irrational, crazy, nuts, whack-job, cray-cray, lunatic, schizo, psycho, or dangerous. The list could go on forever. Despite the fact that, statistically, we are surrounded by people we love or simply interact with who have mental illness, we use strong negative language to describe those who are dealing with mental health issues. The stigmas surrounding the subject continue to do serious harm to those who are struggling, causing many to never seek treatment.

Stigma. What does it mean? Healthplace.com posts this on their website: "According to the *Webster's New World Dictionary*, the short definition of stigma is a mark of disgrace or reproach. Dr. Kristalyn Salters-Pedneault offers this definition of stigma, 'Stigma is a perceived negative attribute that causes someone to devalue or think less of the whole person.' Given these two representations for the meaning of stigma, anyone can see that stigma, of any kind, is a deeply negative mindset and provides no value to society in general."[2]

A rarely used plural form of stigma is stigmata, usually referring to the nail wounds on Christ's hands and feet during the crucifixion. Stigmata are caused by punctures made with a sharp instrument. How does this apply to what I've been saying? Words like 'crazy,' 'nuts,' 'psycho' and 'schizo' hurt – They puncture the soul of people who are struggling just to live. They wound people, families, and society as a whole. Whoever created the phrase, 'sticks and stones will break my bones, but words will never hurt me,' was frankly an idiot. We have all been hurt by words, and admittedly, we have all hurt other people with ours.

Mental Health vs. Mental Illness

Mental health is not mental illness. Mental health, for every one of us, is simply how we think, feel, and act in order to do life. It's how we view ourselves, interact with others, make decisions, and love. It also plays a significant role in how we deal with stress, have relationships with others, make daily choices, and reach life decisions. Mental health affects all of us, because --- even if we sometimes wonder—we all have a brain.

People can have good or not so good mental health. But we've all got it. Mental Health America, the nation's leading community-based non-profit dedicated to addressing the needs of those living with mental illness and promoting the overall mental health of all Americans, states: "Some people think that only people with mental illnesses have to pay attention to their mental health. But the truth is that your emotions, thoughts and attitudes affect your energy, productivity and overall health. Good mental health strengthens your ability to cope with everyday hassles and more serious crises and challenges. Good mental health is essential to creating the life you want.

Just as you brush your teeth or get a flu shot, you can take steps to promote your mental health. A great way to start is by learning to deal with stress.[3]"

Even though they are not the same, the term, "mental health" carries with it some of the same stigmas as the term, "mental illness." For example, quite often an officer will get a "mental health call" over the radio. Sometimes, the call involves someone who may be mentally ill. We hear mental health; we think mental illness. When we say, "Take care of your mental health," others think, "I'm fine. I'm not crazy."

So, what's the difference between mental health and mental illness? The National Alliance on Mental Illness (NAMI), the nation's largest grassroots mental health organization dedicated to building better lives for the millions of Americans affected by mental illness, describes mental illness as "a condition that affects a person's thinking, feeling or mood. Such conditions may affect someone's ability to relate to others and function each day." They go on to add, "A mental health condition isn't the result of one event. Research suggests multiple overlapping causes. Genetics, environment and lifestyle influence whether someone develops a mental health condition. A stressful job or home life makes some people more susceptible, as do traumatic life events like being the victim of a crime. Biochemical processes and circuits and basic brain structure may play a role too."[4]

Key to this definition is the statement that mental illnesses and conditions not only involve genetics, environment, and lifestyle, but also biochemical processes, circuits, and basic brain structure.

The National Council for Behavioral Health defines mental illness as "a diagnosable illness that affects a person's thinking, emotional state, and behavior, and disrupts the person's ability to work, carry out daily activities, and engage in satisfying relationships."[5] The key word in this definition is "diagnosable," meaning that it's a real thing that can be identified and recognized. If mental illness can be diagnosed, it can be treated. If it can be treated, then people can recover from it.

Lack of Diagnosis and Treatment

Here are two startling statistics.

- Estimates suggest that only half of people with mental illnesses receive treatment[6].

- The median length of time a person delays getting treatment from the first time they recognize that there might be a problem is 10 years[7].

What makes these statistics particularly alarming is that mental illnesses are diagnosable medical conditions. Just like diabetes is a disorder of the pancreas, mental illness is a disorder of the brain. However, the brain is a very complex organ—much more complex than your pancreas, liver, or any other organ in your body.

Mental health professionals diagnose mental illnesses by observing and collecting a myriad of signs and symptoms. I can't take a blood test for depression. My doctor and family need to see the signs, and I need to feel the symptoms. This is true not only for depression, but with all other mental illnesses as well. When someone has a broken arm, doctors can take an x-ray, show you on the backlit screen, and point to where it is broken. Not only does it look broken when you look down at it and see your arm pointing in the wrong direction, but it feels broken because it hurts. With all that evidence, you can conclude that your arm is broken and needs treatment.

It's not so easy with mental illness. Professionals diagnose mental illnesses and disorders by gathering a list of signs (what they and others see) and symptoms (what the person themselves is experiencing). The problem with that is, unlike the broken arm, I can hide my signs, fake my way through life, and never talk about how I feel. Therefore, someone can have an untreated mental illness for years, never seek help, and cause a lot of damage along the way to their own lives, and the lives of people they love and love them back.

Going back to my broken arm analogy, imagine if only 50% of people who had a broken arm got help, and it took them 10 years to get it. So, why does this happen with mental illness? I think that the biggest problem with this very under diagnosed and undertreated illness is that it is seen as some kind of character flaw or personal weakness. As I stated, these are the words society, the media, and Hollywood use for mental illness—crazy, nutjob, whack-job, lunatic, and psycho. Or other phrases that describe a person with mental illness like "one fry short of a Happy Meal" and "their elevator doesn't go all the way up to the top floor." Other phrases specific to police include "frequent flier" or "10-78" (or whatever code number your department uses for mental health calls).

Why is this an acceptable way to talk about other human beings? There are lots of reasons, but two on the top of my list is that we make fun of what we don't know about and it makes it easier to distinguish us (healthy people) against them (people with a mental illness).

Contrast that language with the words we use when we talk about people with other medical conditions. We use words like brave, strong, warrior, survivor, and others that reflect strength, courage, and resilience. Those words, which are incredibly true, describe people who are battling a disease or condition that is drastically affecting their life. People with mental illness get "crazy" and "nuts," while people with physical conditions get "heroic" and "fighter." Is there any wonder why only half of individuals get treatment for their mental health? Who wants to be called or labeled, "crazy?" No one.

Since openly discussing my mental illnesses, I have had the opportunity to speak to hundreds of other people who also have these illnesses. To be honest, I have never met stronger, braver, and more courageous people in my life than those who live day to day with mental illness.

Common Reasons People Avoid Treatment

Over the years, I've put together a list of why most people, including law enforcement officers, refuse to seek treatment for their mental health issues. Here are a few common things people say and think:

- **Fear:** "What would people say?" "What will happen to my job?" "What if my chief finds out?" "What if my buddies find out?" "What if there's something really wrong with my head?"

- **Embarrassment/Shame**: "What do I say if I've got to take time off?" "My wife and kids will look down on me." "Who would be proud of me for finding out I'm crazy?" "I'm not one of those people."

- **Hopelessness/Helplessness**: "What's the point?" "There's no help for me anyway." "It's just me feeling stressed out. No big deal."

- **Rejection/Discrimination**: "I will definitely lose friends over this." "Who would want to have coffee with a nutcase?" "Might as well forget about ever getting promoted."

- **I can't afford it:** "Yeah, I have pretty good insurance, but the copays for a therapist and medication are way too expensive." "I work too hard for my money to just give it away."

- **Worthlessness/Expendability:** "I feel completely worthless every day; That's what my ex used to call me." "I've been told every day since the academy that I'm easily replaceable, so I'm not special to anyone. So why get help?"

- **No desire to change**: "I like how I am. Sure, I've been married four times and none of my kids will talk to me, but hey, that's their problem. I think I'm just fine."

- **Denial/Unaware that anything is wrong:** "I'm ok. Not sure what everyone is talking about. I see nothing wrong with having 5-6 beers every night after work." "People say that I'm acting different...It's the world that's different."

Common Myths About Mental Illness

There are so many myths surrounding mental disorders. The consequence is that people do not seek treatment or are subject to stigma when they do. Here are some of the common myths that I have seen over the decades, both as a person with mental illness and as an advocate working to shine light on mental disorders and suicide in law enforcement.

Mental toughness prevents depression, stress, and trauma. Mental toughness and toughening your way through life may work for a while, but as a coping mechanism, it will catch up to you. Granted, some officers can go through an entire career and not be affected by all that they see and do. Some officers, like some people, can be very resilient. They can face the same challenges as everyone else, but instead of it causing mental health issues, they have the ability to bounce back.

That in no way means that some officers are tougher than others. It simply means that some are more resilient. Despite wearing the same uniform, we're all different. We all respond differently to stresses and traumas in our lives. One person may go through a divorce and say, "Thank goodness that's over!" Another would be absolutely devastated.

I can recall a time back around 2002 when we were looking into whether or not we would start issuing tasers to our officers. We decided to try them out to see exactly what they were all about. I had been a defensive tactics instructor for many years, and now I heard other instructors talking about the tasers. They challenged me to get tased. In fact, I was challenged on my ability to take the full "5 second ride"—getting tasered for the five full seconds before it automatically turns off. Not being one to back down, I agreed to do it.

I got myself so amped up for the test that I actually have myself on video talking into the camera like a pro-wrestler getting ready for a match. As the Deputy Chief Alexander and Chief

Duffy watched, several other instructors were tased for one to two seconds. Given their reaction, I knew it hurt. When it was my turn, my scenario was to not only see if I could get tased, but also if I could still get to a rubber knife lying six feet away. Comically, as extra incentive, the Chief threw a $5 bill next to the knife, to see if I could grab that too.

Somebody said, "Go," the taser hit me, and I went down to my knees. I crawled across the mats—the video shows sparks coming from my shirt – and struggled desperately to grab the knife. I got it and started stabbing at someone's boot in front of me as the taser operator screamed commands to drop the knife. After five seconds, when the taser shuts off automatically, I rose up on my knees with knife still in hand and started stabbing toward the officer again. Verbal commands continued as I got tased again. This lasted another three seconds until I could no longer take it, threw the knife away, and laid face down with my arms spread out. I finally gave up. Instructors were checking the taser to make sure the batteries were in right, because what I did wasn't supposed to be able to happen. I took nearly eight seconds of being tased. And yes, I also took the $5.

Why am I telling you this story? Please know that I am not telling you this to sound cool. Why I am telling you this is that my entire technique for getting tased was to simply tough it out and psyche myself up so much that I wouldn't allow the taser to affect me. It worked for nearly eight seconds, but then it beat me. I gave up and couldn't take it anymore. Why I am telling you this is for my first 16 years in law enforcement, I tried the same technique every day. I would just tough my way through it, creating in myself a mentality that would allow nothing to affect me. And it worked, right up until it didn't. Right up until the time I first told my wife that I wanted to kill myself. Mental toughness might prolong the issues of depression, stress, and trauma, but it absolutely doesn't prevent it.

Mental Illness is a sign of weakness and lack of character. I've talked about this earlier in the chapter, but it bears repeating. This myth causes so many people to be afraid of seeking help. Mental illness is a medical condition, not a sign of weakness. Do we say that cancer is a sign of weakness? Of course not. The same argument holds true for mental illness being caused by lack of character.

This doesn't happen to people like us. Mental illnesses can affect persons of *any* age, race, religion, income, or occupation. I've often said that we know that very few police officers will ever be involved in a police shooting sometime in their career. So, why do we bother to wear a vest and carry a gun? The answer is obvious. You wear a vest and carry a gun because you never know. Statistically, you have a high probability of never having to use it. But I wouldn't go to work without them, talking about how it won't happen to me. The same is true for mental illness. One can't be so arrogant to think that they are immune.

They are simply not trying hard enough to handle life's problems. So many times, people would say to me, "Just try harder" or "Why can't you just be happy?" Imagine if we said to somebody going through chemotherapy, "You know why the chemo is not working, don't you? You're not trying hard enough. If you just sat there and really concentrated, it might work better." How absolutely ridiculous does that sound? "Just try harder." When it comes to mental health disorders, trying harder for some people is simply getting out of bed in the morning.

Snap out of it and pull yourself together. A person can't snap out of anxiety, depression, or any other mental illness any more than someone can snap out of diabetes.

People choose to be depressed. Is it true that there are miserable people in the world? Yes. But I'm not talking about people who just choose to be miserable. A person doesn't wake up one day and say, "Life is too good for me. Let me try having panic attacks for a while." I didn't choose mental illness. I honestly would much rather have something else, but that is what I have. I don't want it and don't like it, but I have it.

Real men/women don't have those kinds of problems. In law enforcement, this is a huge myth. Since policing is typically a very male dominated profession, many officers believe that "real men" don't experience mental illness. I guess it all depends on what your definition of what a real man is. My definition of a real man used to be someone who used a lot of force, had affairs, swore, drank, bullied people, and so on. It wasn't until I realized what the actual definition of a real man was—the opposite of my past beliefs—that I really could start getting the help I needed. Many female officers experience and feel similarly as well.

If I admit that I am stressed, people will think I'm weak and lazy. Again, this boils down to being afraid of what people think of you. Many of us have fears that prevent us from doing anything to help ourselves because someone might find out. Here's the irony. My old department, like any other department, has a turnover rate when people retire, and new recruits are hired. In the last 15 years since my retirement, probably 200 to 300 new officers have come into the department. That means that there are probably 200-300 police officers or more in the city of Rochester who have never heard of Eric Weaver. Even though I gave my blood, sweat and tears for more than two decades just like so many officers, after you retire, a whole group of people won't even know your name. So, who's still going to be around after we retire? Our kids, family, partner, and all the people we blew off when we put our jobs and what other officers' thought about us ahead of what was really important—our life outside of the job.

I'll be fine; it's not that bad. Imagine that you fall down the stairs and your femur is sticking out through your thigh.

Would you say, "I'm going to be okay, I'm just going to walk it off, I'm just going to toughen it out, I'll be all right?" Of course not. You're going to get some help. With mental illness and just talking about problems, we tend to say, "I'll be okay, and I'll be alright—just having a bad day, bad month, bad year." At some point, many of us need to realize that things simply don't get better on their own. How much worse do you want things to get before you reach out for help?

People with a mental illness have a diminished intelligence level. Contrary to what people might believe, mental illness has nothing to do with intelligence. Mental illness and developmental or intellectual disabilities are not the same things. There are countless men and women with mental illness that are extremely intelligent and very successful. In fact, there is evidence that high intelligence may actually be connected to mental illness.

In one research study, a team of researchers surveyed 3,715 members of American Mensa with an IQ higher than 130. They were asked to report mood and anxiety disorders, or whether they suspected that they suffered from any mental illnesses that had yet to be diagnosed. After comparing this with the statistical national average for each illness, the researchers found that those in the Mensa community had considerably higher rates of varying disorders[8].

People should deal with their problems without taking pills. Mental illness is a medical condition. For many people, treatment requires medication, and that needs to be okay. There are thousands of officers that are on mental health medication that their departments don't even know about. Unfortunately, for many more, instead of actually going to a professional and getting help, we just go to the bar and self-medicate with alcohol. We need to create a law enforcement culture that openly discusses this issue, as opposed to, "Don't take a pill. Let's just go have a drink." Many people have the misconception that once you're on a medication you'll be on it for the rest of your life, which is simply not always the case. There may be times that medication is only used for a very short term. It all depends on the individual and the circumstances surrounding it.

I was interviewed for an article in a newspaper back in 2006 in which I was asked my opinion about a deputy in a large west coast police department, that had just been fired because her superiors found out she was bipolar and on medication. The officer put some paperwork in the internal mail to request time off because she had bipolar disorder and was under a doctor's care. Her doctor had made a change in her medication, and the officer needed to be able to take some extra days off, as allowed under federal law, should the switch prove troublesome. Days later, her gun and badge were taken away after more than six years on the force. Her administration said that they had to protect the public.

I told them that my department took a different approach. I was supported by my agency's top administrators and returned to duty after my hospitalizations while on multiple medications. I told the writer that what their administration said to entire department was essentially this: "If you've got a problem, we better damn well not find out about it because if we do, you're gone. Keep your problems to yourself." Or, "We'll find you unfit for duty and a liability." That was the message, loud and clear. After all, what would happen if an officer was involved in a high-profile incident and was found to be on medication for depression?

Today, I tell administrations around the country that I would much rather have an officer who was getting professional help and treatment on appropriate mental health medication, than an officer who gets drunk every night and uses unhealthy self-medicating coping skills to get through life. Mental disorder medication for millions of people, including law enforcement officers, is generally safe and effective and allows people to live happier, healthier, and more productive lives. Also, medication alone is rarely the sole treatment for a mental health condition. Common professional and personal experience tells us that medication, along with proper and appropriate therapy, achieves the best outcome for those living with mental health related issues.

I don't want to be one of "those people." Remember the number – one out of five people. Many of us, including family members, are "those people." As I already mentioned, mental illnesses can affect persons of any age, race, religion, income, or occupation.

Conclusion

Although more resources and educational materials are available today than ever before, many of the stigmas and myths about mental illness remain the same. As more people become public about the effect of mental illness on their lives and treatment they are receiving, the dialogue opens up and stigmas and myths lose their power. Throughout history, this has happened with many physical diseases like tuberculosis, leprosy, cancer, and AIDs. It has happened with alcoholism and drug addiction. The best way to overcome these stigmas is to not believe or promote them among your co-workers and family.

As I mentioned, it is my belief that the statistic that one out of five people has a mental disorder is not accurate for law enforcement officers. I believe that the number is higher. Certainly, there are professions that experience lots of trauma, such as firefighters, EMS personnel, ER doctors and nurses, but the general public is not subjected to the cumulative stress and trauma experienced by law enforcement.

CHAPTER 7

UNDERSTANDING DEPRESSION

I was diagnosed with major depressive disorder through most of my early hospitalizations and after I began therapy in 1995. At home, I didn't want to get out of bed, was tired all the time, and felt like I was stuck in quicksand that was sucking the life out of me. At work, I put on a great show even though I was infinitely sad. I didn't care about anybody and believed they felt the same about me. And I was angry, so incredibly angry. I didn't know then that depression, especially in men, often reveals itself in the form of anger. My depression quickly caused me to turn to thoughts of taking my own life as I began to believe that suicide couldn't be worse than how I was feeling.

Depression is a very powerful illness. Contrary to what many people believe, it's more than just feeling sad or having a bad day or week. We all have been sad, and we will all be sad again over and over in our lives. That, however, doesn't necessarily mean you have a depressive disorder, which can only be diagnosed by a professional. Actual depression is when sadness just doesn't seem to go away; it can be a serious mental health condition, affecting every aspect of your life. More than 17 million adults in the U.S. (seven percent of the population) experience at least one major depressive episode yearly, regardless of their age, ethnicity, gender or socioeconomic background.[1]

When depression is not recognized or treated, it can lead to a very difficult and destructive time for the individual going through it, as well as for the people who love and care for them. Left untreated, it can destroy lives, relationships, and families. Individuals may lash out or avoid people all together, as well as self-medicate with a variety of unhealthy coping strategies. Like any mental illness, depressive disorder is a diagnosable medical condition that disrupts a person's thinking, feelings, moods, ability to relate to others, and daily functioning. Many people will have only one major episode of depression in their lives, but the consequences, if untreated, can be significant. Others will experience reoccurrences with episodes often lasting longer each time.

Causes of Depression

Depression does not have a single cause. It can be triggered by a life crisis, physical illness or something else, as well as occur spontaneously. The National Alliance on Mental Illness offers the following as a list of causes of depression[2]:

- **Trauma.** When people experience trauma at an early age, it can cause long-term changes in how their brains respond to fear and stress. These changes may lead to depression.

- **Genetics.** Mood disorders, such as depression, tend to run in families.

- **Life circumstances**. Marital status, relationship changes, financial standing and where a person lives influence whether a person develops depression.

- **Brain changes**. Imaging studies have shown that the frontal lobe of the brain becomes less active when a person is depressed. Depression is also associated with changes in how the pituitary gland and hypothalamus respond to hormone stimulation. Brain changes can also occur with Traumatic Brain Injury (TBI).

- **Other medical conditions.** People who have a history of sleep disturbances, medical illness, chronic pain, anxiety and attention-deficit hyperactivity disorder (ADHD) are more likely to develop depression. Some medical syndromes like hypothyroidism can mimic depressive disorder. Additionally, some medications can cause symptoms of depression.

- **Drug and alcohol misuse.** Fifty percent of adults with a substance use disorder also experienced a mental health related issue[3]. Co-occurring disorders require coordinated treatment for both conditions, as alcohol can worsen depressive symptoms.

Common Signs and Symptoms of Depression

Professionals look at signs and symptoms to diagnose depression. A sign is what people can see or observe in someone else, such as excessive sleeping or being tearful. A symptom is what the individual is feeling, such as sadness or anger. What shows itself as a depression in one person may not look like depression in someone else because we are all unique. Interestingly, when you look at the common signs and symptoms of depression, they look quite a bit like those I'll discuss relating to both suicide and cumulative stress. Remember, a trained professional can only diagnose depressive disorder. To be diagnosed with depressive disorder, a person must have experienced a depressive episode lasting longer than two weeks.

There are common signs and symptoms that you can look for in yourself and those around you. Here are several:

- **Changes in sleep.** During the peak of my depression, I slept constantly. What does a child often do when they don't want to get up and go to school? Pull the blanket over their head. Adults do the same thing, either literally or figuratively. What happened when I would come up from under the blanket? I had to face the world and my problems. If I could just pull the blanket back over my head, I didn't have to face any of it. I could escape in sleep. Other people become so depressed that they are unable to sleep at all. Excessive worry, guilt, hopelessness, or other distressing thoughts cause many to never sleep, as they continually attempt to resolve their issues in their minds.

- **Changes in appetite.** Many people self-medicate their depression with food by either eating more than usual, or not eating at all. An excessive or unusual gain or loss of weight can indicate depression.

- **Lack of concentration.** Often, the inability to focus on work or family can be a symptom of depression. It is not because a person isn't trying; concentrating on one or two specific things can feel almost impossible.

- **Loss of energy/fatigue.** This can often co-occur with changes in sleep or appetite. Realistically, as I mentioned earlier, law enforcement isn't necessarily a physically demanding job. But how many of us come home from work and are just mentally and physically exhausted? Again, depression can make you feel like you are stuck in mud or quicksand. Constant fatigue along with loss of energy leading to excessive sleeping can be a major sign of depression.

- **Lack of interest in activities.** There is a long list of signs relating to lack of interest and not finding any pleasure or joy from the activities of life that a person normally cares about. For example, no longer wanting to go to your son's soccer games, no longer showing interest in your favorite football or baseball teams, or simply not wanting to be involved with anything that used to not just make you happy, but bring you joy.

- **Physical aches and pains.** Depression can lead to headaches, muscle soreness, backaches, and more. Remember that mental illnesses, such as depression, are medical conditions that can affect the body as a whole.

- **Excessive anger, irritability, or agitation**. Often, we think of depression as, "I'm just going to sit down and cry." That's true, but there are other powerful emotions that can quickly become out of control because they are easy to express. We have a lot of officers, both men and women, who have severe anger issues and are quick to get agitated and irritated with everyone and everything around them. It is my belief that what we actually have are officers who are clinically depressed; they just don't know that how they are acting and feeling may actually be depression.

- **Use of drugs or alcohol.** Just like food or sleep, drugs and alcohol can be a coping mechanism to help people deal with depression. They can become an unhealthy coping mechanism, and many people begin to self-medicate with one or both of these because they believe it will help them feel better. In reality, people are using them to not feel at all.

- **Suicidal thoughts**. I will discuss this issue in great length, but no longer wanting to live is a major sign and symptom of depression. Most people who die by suicide were dealing with some type of depression (diagnosed or undiagnosed) at the time of their death.

One important note is that the signs and symptoms of depression such as lack of energy, loss of interest, and loss of concentration can often be judged by your fellow officers, your spouse, and even yourself as laziness. Not wanting to take calls, blowing off reports, calling in sick, not wanting to do cell checks, or not wanting to do household chores is not necessarily always simply laziness. I'm certainly not saying that everyone who is lazy is depressed; I know that there are many lazy officers, husbands and wives out there, just like there are lazy doctors, lawyers or Uber drivers. But what looks like laziness to many, may actually be depression. If these signs or symptoms become more and more evident in you or in someone else, it is time to openly talk with a professional.

Treating Depression

Although depressive disorder can be a devastating illness, it often responds to treatment. The key is to get a specific evaluation and treatment plan as well as a safety plan for individuals who have suicidal thoughts. After an assessment rules out medical and other possible causes, a patient-centered treatment plan can include any or a combination of the following [4]:

- **Psychotherapy,** including cognitive behavioral therapy, family-focused therapy and interpersonal therapy.

- **Psychoeducation and Support Group**s - Psychoeducation involves teaching individuals about their illness, how to treat it, and how to recognize signs of relapse. Family psychoeducation is also helpful for family members who want to understand what their loved one is experiencing.

- **Medications,** including antidepressants, mood stabilizers and antipsychotic medications.

- **Exercise** can help with prevention and mild-to-moderate symptoms.

- **Brain stimulation therapies** can be tried if psychotherapy and/or medication are not effective. These include electroconvulsive therapy (ECT) for depressive disorder with psychosis, or repetitive transcranial magnetic stimulation (RTMS) for severe depression.

- **Alternative approaches,** including acupuncture, meditation, faith, and nutrition can be part of a comprehensive treatment plan.

- **Experimental Treatments** such as ketamine and deep brain stimulation are treatments that are not FDA-approved, but are being researched.

How to Help Someone with Depression

Untreated depression can destroy relationships, families and careers. Fortunately, depression is very treatable. The biggest challenge is getting a person to openly discuss it, whether with a primary care doctor or significant other. Most often, people dealing with depression will primarily discuss their physical symptoms such as aches, pains, or headaches. Much of this is due to stigma; there is no stigma discussing headaches with your doctor or family. There is, however, stigma associated with talking about how you can't stop crying. If you or someone you care about is showing signs and symptoms of this common illness of depression, it is important to have open and honest discussions.

It is also important to understand that there are many difficult challenges and experiences families and friends face when a loved one is dealing with depression. It is often difficult to not be affected by the individual's behavior, such as withdrawing from activities, creating distance both emotionally and physically, and behaving in unpredictable ways. Regardless, you truly can help someone who is caught up in this mental illness while taking care of yourself.

- **Recognize the signs and symptoms early on:** Depression has many signs and symptoms, and if addressed and discussed early, it may help the individual tremendously. Like any other illness, early intervention is important. It allows the person to get the help and treatment they need before it turns into a crisis situation.

- **Remain calm and non-judgmental:** If an individual's situation does turn into a crisis, remain calm and listen without judgment to your loved one. Then take whatever steps necessary to get them help and keep them safe. We can easily get frustrated with ourselves or loved ones and say something like, "Here we go again. Are you kidding me? Another day just lying around the house?" That, of course, is the opposite thing we should be saying.

- **Connect with the person:** Openly discuss what you are seeing and take time to listen to what they are saying. Depression can be caused by a variety of factors, including actual medical ones as listed above. Do not tell the person to "just be happy" or ask them "what do they have to be sad about?" Ask them how you can help them or offer some suggestions as to how you can help. Most importantly, make sure the person knows that you truly care about them.

- **Make sure you practice your own self-care:** Caring for someone with depression can be exhausting for families, loved ones, and friends. Frustration, irritation, and even anger on the part of the caregiver are very real. Learn ways to positively talk about your own thoughts and feelings with others who will listen and provide positive feedback and support. Getting support for yourself is essential to be able to help the person you care about.

Depression is real. It is not weakness, laziness, or any other of those stigmatizing words society throws around. Untreated depression can lead to many things, including suicide. If you, a loved one, fellow officer, or anyone you care about appears depressed, acknowledge it and find supportive treatment.

CHAPTER 8

PATHWAYS OF STRESS AND TRAUMA

Our sensitivity to stress gets collectively heighted by many events, including 9/11, tragic mass shootings, the coronavirus, line-of-duty and off-duty deaths of a fellow officer or friend, and civil unrest. All of these, and countless others, that are associated with our profession on a daily basis, lead to a type of stress that not many other occupations face. For many people, trauma and stress can be amplified way beyond their normal jobs, and one possible silver-lining aspect of those experiences is that they somehow and in some way heighten society's collective awareness and empathy for those who experience cumulative stress and trauma on a regular basis.

So, what exactly is stress? Stress is a state of mental or emotional strain or tension resulting from adverse or very demanding circumstances[1]. There are both negative and positive stressors. Some positive stressors include getting married, earning a promotion, having a baby, or buying a house. These are all stressful, but we anticipate a positive outcome. They are also time-limited with a finite ending. We have the wedding, start the new job, give birth, or close on the house. Negative stressors, which will be one of the focuses on this chapter, tend to linger and work negatively on our lives if not properly addressed.

Stressors can cause anxiety. We may be anxious about not knowing what to do or whether we have the abilities to accomplish a task. Anxiety isn't necessarily bad; it can actually be a good thing. Anxiety can help save our lives, push us to study harder, and drive us into achieving more. Stressors can also trigger a fight or flight response. When we perceive a threat, our bodies become challenged by that situation. Our culture is built on the stories of the runaway bride (flight) or the hero mom who overcame all odds to rescue her child (fight). In addition to fight or flight, we can also respond by freezing or not being able to respond at all.

In law enforcement, we generally do not have the option of flight or freeze. In reality, we sometimes flee or take flight, but we don't ever use those words. Instead we call it a 'tactical retreat'—much cooler than describing it as flight. During a rare tactical retreat, we remove ourselves from the area, regroup, and then go back in again. In law enforcement, we also experience burst stress. Burst stress occurs when you're sitting in your car or officer's desk, and suddenly a call comes in for shots fired or a fight in cellblock 2. What happens to your adrenaline and heart rate? They increase and remain high, until the situation is resolved, and your body starts to calm down. Then 20 minutes later, you get a call about a man with a knife or a sexual assault on campus. It's burst stress again, and this repeated cycle takes a toll on us emotionally, mentally and physically throughout our careers. Combine that with poor diet and lack of exercise, and the potential for some real physical problems is pretty evident. And even though it is a very human reaction to stress, law enforcement officers don't have the luxury to freeze or not act. Inaction by an officer, or simply not acting fast enough during an event can result in media scrutiny, outrage, and even termination.

Over the years, I have found a very useful model[2] for talking about stress in the classes I teach – explaining the pathways of stress. Essentially, police officers experience stress through two different routes -- normal pathways and destructive pathways.

Other professionals also experience stress along normal and destructive pathways in occupations like health care, the military and firefighting, but we will be focusing on law enforcement primarily. In fact, people in the general population can also go down these pathways in situations of abuse, violence, or man-made and natural disasters.

Normal Pathway: General Stress

General stress falls under normal pathways. General stress is not a surprise idea for anyone; it's what we consider typical to everyday life. We all deal with it. We have bills to pay, kids to get to soccer games, and arguments with our spouses. Sometimes, the stress is negative and sometimes it's positive, but all of it is manageable. That's the key word – manageable. Most of the time with general stress, people will recover from it, stay healthy, and even grow and learn how to deal with the situation better next time.

Sometimes, people do not appropriately deal with general stress, whether they are civilians or in law enforcement. Then it can easily move into a destructive pathway and lead to *cumulative stress*, which I will talk about shortly. For a police officer, general stress under a normal pathway is different because of his or her occupation. In addition to having the bills, kids, and spouse stressors, they also have the stress that comes with a job that can be dangerous, demoralizing, and disturbing.

Normal Pathway: Critical Incident Stress

In law enforcement, critical incident stress is also on the normal pathway. Also called traumatic stress, it is caused by exposure to a severe, overwhelming or even frightening situation that is beyond ordinary human experience. As officers, we don't have to be on the job too long to realize that we come into a lot of contact with things that are truly beyond ordinary human experience. If we worked most places outside of law enforcement or corrections, we know that we wouldn't be seeing the things that we see. Ordinary human experiences do not generally involve abused or dead children, suicides, severe assaults, homicide scenes, or fatal car accidents. It is important to understand that it is normal to have a painful response to these experiences, and that a painful response is how normal, healthy people respond to an abnormal event. For the most part, most of us entering law enforcement are normal, healthy people who have families and loved ones. We work, however, in an occupation that creates lots of abnormal events, and we face these critical incidents day after day, year and year.

We experience a variety of symptoms as the result of critical incident stress. Some can be physical like heart palpitations or exhaustion. We may experience depression or distorted thinking. We may have changes in behavior like outbursts of anger. When properly dealt with, most people recover from critical incident stress and remain healthy and productive. When the effects of a critical incident lasts beyond four weeks and is not being taken care of, it can turn into a much more serious problem called *post-traumatic stress disorder.*

The important words here are, "properly dealt with." How do we properly deal with critical incident stress? One answer is, debriefing. As I have mentioned, in my day, "debriefing" wasn't a word that anybody even heard of. Today, we know that debriefings are helping a lot of officers in difficult situations. Unfortunately, they are not happening nearly as much as they should. While debriefings are often held with major critical incidents such as police shootings, unless you have a supervisor who truly believes in debriefing in some way or another, it may not happen for what is considered more minor critical incidents. Other answers are peer counseling, EAP, talking with your primary care doctor, creating and doing positive coping skills, and so many other things that are *productive,* not *destructive,* as we are so prone to doing.

Destructive Pathway: Cumulative Stress

Cumulative stress falls under destructive pathway, and is often referred to as burnout; an intense state of physical and mental exhaustion. Everyone has experienced normal mental and physical exhaustion. We're tired, and we don't want to hear about the kids, the bills, or anything our spouses have to say. We are just plain tired. We get a good night's sleep, have a weekend off, or even take a vacation, and that exhaustion is reduced or goes away. In cumulative stress or burnout, severe exhaustion doesn't leave, and it is generally not caused by intense physical activity. Let's face it. As police officers, our jobs are not really that physically demanding. We might get into a fight with someone every once in a while, but we're not out there blacktopping driveways, digging ditches, and building bridges. Instead, we are doing a lot of things over and over again that cause us to have mental exhaustion, which can in turn feel like physical exhaustion.

Cumulative stress occurs as a result of prolonged exposure to a great many stressors. What is prolonged exposure? Is it a month, six months, five years or 20 years? And what counts as great many stressors? From discussions with thousands of officers, I have made these two observations: First, experiencing cumulative stress depends on the person in terms of how many stressors, what kind of stressors, and how prolonged a time. Too many stressors for me might not be too many stressors to you. Every one of us is different, and that's such an important thing to realize when it comes to stress. We handle stress differently in a way that works for us, or what we think works for us.

A sergeant came up to me and said, "Eric, you talk about this stress and burnout stuff. I have one cop who's been in the job six months telling me how burned out he is. I've been doing this job for 12 years, and I'm not burned out. I absolutely know he's not burned out." I asked him how he knew. "He isn't burned out because he's been on the job only six months. What can he have possibly done to be burned out? So, I told him to come back to me in 11 and a half years and then tell me how burned out he was. Until then, go do your job." I answered the sergeant firmly, "How do you know he wasn't burned out? He's not you. You don't know anything about his life. Do you know anything about him, his family, or what's going on to cause him to say that? Do you know anything at all about this young officer after six months?" The truth is that too often in law enforcement, we mistakenly compare ourselves with others. "If this doesn't bother me, then it shouldn't bother you. I've been doing this job for 20 years, and I'm fine. You've been doing this job for two. What's your problem? What's wrong with you? Get over it."

I have also observed that cumulative stress is often a combination of work and non-work-related stressors. Many of us have an argument at home and end up reacting negatively at work. We give out an unnecessary ticket, take it out on an inmate or argue with a fellow officer. The same thing happens when we have a bad day at work and bring it home to take out on somebody we love. It happens all too often. We will talk about this more in depth later when we discuss relationships. Just let me say that this is a huge issue in law enforcement families. When someone tells me that they always leave work at work, I respond with, "If you can do that, please bottle it up and sell it because I don't know how you do that."

Many people ask what finally caused me to talk with my wife about suicide in 1995. The answer has been pretty clear—cumulative stress and trauma. I experienced a build-up of work and non-work-related stressors, childhood and teenage issues, police traumas and many different things that happened over a period of time. What actually caused the moment I reached out to her? I really don't know. Remember, stressors don't need to be necessarily severe to activate cumulative stress. A minor motor vehicle accident or something as simple as putting someone in isolation can trigger cumulative stress and trauma. It's not necessarily that particular stressor that caused cumulative stress to happen. It's almost like the last straw, realizing that if you take one more thing – even the smallest, simplest of things, you won't be able to function.

Cumulative stress can impair or block your ability to perform at work or at home. At work, you can find yourself sitting in the parking lot for as many hours as possible so not to answer a job, hiding someplace, or not taking backups. At home, it can be not talking to your wife, playing with your children, or doing chores around the house. Cumulative stress can actually alter your personality. You can actually start acting like a different person to the point where others ask the question, "Who are you?" All of a sudden your spouse can say, "I don't even know who you are anymore. You do and say things that are not like the person I married." In the next chapter, I will talk in detail about the phases of cumulative stress and what can be done to stop it from impairing your ability to perform at work and home.

Destructive Pathway: Post-Traumatic Stress Disorder

The final pathway is post-traumatic stress (PTS), when people are exposed to or witness events that overwhelm their coping and problem-solving abilities. It's simply beyond what we know how to deal with, experience or understand. However, not everyone who experiences PTS will go on to have PTSD. PTSD is a mental illness, a diagnosable psychiatric disorder that can occur in people who have experienced or witnessed a traumatic event such as a natural disaster, a serious accident, a terrorist act, war/combat, rape or other violent personal assault. PTSD knows no boundaries of gender, ethnicity, or age.

The following statistics are based on the U.S. population[3]:

- About 7 or 8 out of every 100 people (or 7-8% of the population) will have PTSD at some point in their lives.

- About 8 million adults have PTSD during a given year. This is only a small portion of those who have experienced a traumatic event.

- About 10 of every 100 women (or 10%) develop PTSD sometime in their lives, compared with about 4 of every 100 men (or 4%).

It's important to note that PTSD isn't only caused by actually experiencing a traumatic event. It can also be caused by exposure to the event. Many individuals who watched the terrorist attacks on 9/11 over and over again on TV dealt with Post Traumatic Stress. It can also be caused by repeated exposure to trauma, which is often the case in officers. My heart has always gone out to that very special investigator whose task it is to investigate sex trafficking and child pornography. Imagine what it is like to see case after case and video after video of child abuse and conduct interviews with those children. Long after the trauma occurs, PTSD causes intense, disturbing thoughts and feelings relating to the experience. People often talk about reliving the event through flashbacks or nightmares. They may feel acute sadness, fear, and anger. Often, they become detached from people around them. Sometimes they experience strong negative reactions to normal occurrences like noise or touch. PTSD is so critical to the topic of mental illness and law enforcement that I have devoted a separate chapter to it later in this book.

A Brief Look at Vicarious Trauma

In addition to the pathways model that I just discussed, I'd like to conclude by talking about another form of trauma – vicarious trauma. Here is an excellent definition from The Vicarious Trauma Institute in Scottsdale: "Vicarious trauma is a transformation in the helper's inner sense of identity and existence that results from utilizing controlled empathy when listening to clients' trauma-content narratives."[4]

In other words, vicarious trauma affects cognitive, physical, psychological, emotional and spiritual health when day after day, someone listens to or responds to traumatic situations while staying in control of their reactions. This transformation changes their perception of the world and can result in depression and anxiety. Simply, with vicarious trauma, we don't necessarily experience the trauma, but it can nonetheless be just as debilitating. The authors of *Second-Hand Shock* provide a useful analogy:

"We've all heard of second-hand smoke. Put yourself in a room with a heavy smoker. You breathe in the smoky air. It irritates your nose, your mouth, your lungs and your blood stream. After a while, you might start wheezing, coughing, and your eyes might become irritated. It will become difficult for you to breathe. Prolonged exposure will adversely affect your health and well-being, causing damage to your heart and your brain. The experience of absorbing trauma, second-hand, is much the same as inhaling second-hand smoke. Helping people in trauma day after day is a contaminant that, if left unaddressed, can kill you. Bearing witness to someone else's trauma is dangerous."[5]

Anyone in law enforcement can relate to this description. Second hand or vicarious trauma is an overwhelming part of our lives. We are exposed to it day after day, year after year, and it is considered part of the job. We see, hear, and experience beyond what the typical person experiences. Certainly, law enforcement is not the only occupation that experiences vicarious trauma. Other occupations such as doctors, nurses, therapists, social workers, EMS personnel, and the clergy can experience it as well. But I believe we witness and are exposed to it on a whole other level than other occupations. We respond to calls that bring us into some of the most violent of circumstances. We see it up close and personal. We are inside homes and jail cells where we see conditions, experience smells, hear the cries of children and crime victims, and get a full sense of horrific situations first-hand.

Equally important, we are required to control our reactions. In a response to a child abuse call where a child is injured and the suspect is present, we—even though we may want to—can't react in a way most people would want to just because that's what he might deserve. Remaining calm, controlling our emotions, and not being able to react the way our human nature may want us to, can actually magnify the vicarious trauma we experience. Ironically, we also expose each other to vicarious trauma through cop humor and by sharing stories to relieve stress. As I have discussed before, our age-old technique of passing each other's trauma back and forth to one another doesn't work. We expose each other and our families to continued vicarious trauma. I have become acutely aware of this danger and become very careful about how and what I share.

Please don't confuse vicarious trauma with simply sharing memories or talking about the old days. What I don't do anymore is provide graphic, vivid, and explicit details of my experiences with someone who is not trained in how to appropriately help me process them. I talk to my therapist who, by the way, is also at serious risk of vicarious trauma. In fact, I often ask her if she is practicing good self-care herself because of all the things she hears. With the exception of some of the stories I mentioned in earlier chapters, such as the attempted suicide I encountered when I worked in the jail, or the lieutenant who offered me cookies from the table where someone had just killed themselves, I carefully choose stories like these when they make a point that can't be made in any other way as effectively. My main reason for discretion, since I am a very direct and open person, is that I don't want to trigger others. At the end of the day, I really don't know where that person is mentally or emotionally, or what they may have experienced in their life. It is my responsibility – as well as any other person in law enforcement – not to contribute to vicarious trauma.

CHAPTER 9

PHASES OF CUMULATIVE STRESS

Imagine you bought a new car and live in a place where there's salt used because of the weather. A couple of years go by, and you notice a little brown corroded spot on the front fender. The first thing you need to do is recognize what it is. If you don't recognize it as rust in the first place, you're probably not going to do much about it. Once you recognize it as rust, you have a few choices—fix it, let it go, or spray paint over it. If you fix it early on, it will be a simple and easy repair. If you let it go, that little rust spot will turn into a bigger one. If you spray paint over it and make it look good on the outside, the rust will still be there, but you'll have disguised it as something it's not and simply covered it up. I remember an old truck that I used to have years ago. When I bought it, the back bumper had been painted black. As it aged, the rust that had been painted over began to seep through. So, I just painted over it again. It looked like new, but the rust was still there, just hidden under a coat of paint. Over time, if never addressed properly, you may eventually just end up driving a rusty mobile.

This is a useful analogy when thinking about cumulative stress – the earlier we deal with things, the better the outcome. Problems don't go away. The analogy, however, does breaks down with the last option – I could always just get a new car. But I can't just get a new me. I'm it. You and I get one shot at life. We can't simply trade ourselves in unless we make some serious changes in our lives. That's why dealing with cumulative stress early on is so important.

Since 2003, when I started teaching class on police stress, I have used a model designed by Jeffrey T. Mitchell, Ph.D., and Grady P. Bray, Ph.D. in their 1990 book, *Emergency Services Stress: Guidelines for Preserving the Health and Careers of Emergency Personnel[1]*. I had the privilege of being trained by Dr. Bray in critical incident stress debriefing in April 2004. Although I have added additional warning signs in each of the phases over the years, the concept of these phases is invaluable. As discussed in the previous chapter and defined by Dr. Bray and Dr. Mitchell's model, cumulative stress:

1. Occurs as a result of prolonged exposure to a great many stressors over a long period of time.

2. Is usually caused by a combination of a wide range of work and non-work-related stressors, which do not necessarily have to be severe.

3. Is often caused by a buildup of unresolved general stress.

4. Is often referred to as 'burnout', a state of mental and physical exhaustion.

5. May often impair or block ability to perform at work and at home.

6. May strain personal and work relationships, and may alter an officer's personality.

So how do we stop cumulative stress from becoming the "rust" that deteriorates our minds, body and soul? How can we recognize the warning signs and take action for ourselves, our family, and the people we work with? Using this model, we can look at cumulative stress in terms of four phases:

- Phase 1: Warning
- Phase 2: Mild Symptoms

- Phase 3: Entrenched Cumulative Stress Reaction
- Phase 4: Severe Debilitating Cumulative Stress Reaction

Phase 1: Warning

The following are six signals or warnings of cumulative stress:

1. Vague anxiety

2. Depression

3. Boredom

4. Apathy

5. Emotional fatigue

6. Loss of sense of humor

We have all experienced some of these at one time or another. Let's start with vague *anxiety*. Has anyone ever asked you what's wrong, and your answer is, "I don't know,"? You realize that you're not quite sure what the problem is, but something isn't right. You just can't put it into words. Many of us have little kids or teenagers and when we ask them to tell us what's going on, they just shrug their shoulders and say, "I don't know" because they don't have the vocabulary to tell us. Adults do the exact same thing. The second warning sign is *depression*. I discussed depression earlier in this book, but as you may remember from that chapter, it is more than just sadness. We start to lose joy in life and the things that made us happy. We no longer look forward to coming home to our kids and getting a big hug from our three-year-old.

How about the third warning sign of cumulative stress – *boredom*? Have you been bored out of your mind at work, despite dealing with shootings, stabbings and fights? Let's face it. For the most part, law enforcement can be a rather monotonous job. We might deal with different people, but it's almost the same thing every day, just different situations. But boredom with cumulative stress goes beyond occasionally not being excited by your work. It is an overall feeling where everything seems dull and tedious. The same is true of the fourth warning sign—*apathy*. Just contrast it with sympathy and empathy. With sympathy, you feel sorry for someone. With empathy, you identify with someone's feelings. But apathy is completely the opposite. You simply just don't care.

Your spouse wants to know what you want to do on your night off, and you immediately respond, "I don't care." When apathy kicks in, it's not that you don't have a preference; it's that you really don't care. With apathy, you start becoming "care-less," not the kind where you trip and fall, but caring less about your life, family, and job. You often move into the fifth warning sign without even realizing it. You become emotionally fatigued. You have no energy, emotionally, to interact and connect with people and your life in general. Emotions simply exhaust you.

The last warning sign of cumulative stress is losing your sense of humor. My daughters loved to tell me knock-knock jokes. "Daddy, knock, knock." "Who's there?" "Chair." "Chair who?" "Rocking chair, hahaha." "Yes, that's real funny," I would respond without even cracking a smile. "Now go tell your mother." It didn't take my daughters long to realize that daddy didn't laugh at things anymore. No matter how hard they tried to make me, I could not. One time when I was in the hospital, my daughters brought me a present they called, "Daddy's Happy Book." They had punched holes in a pile of paper and put it together with yarn. Inside, they pasted pictures of me smiling in an attempt to actually get me to smile again. When I look back, their effort was just heart-breaking. It makes me realize how much joy I lost even with my own kids, and how it affected them. That rust part was really showing.

So, what can we do during Phase 1? Most importantly, we can take these warning signs as the need for intervention. I can notice rust all day long, but if I don't do something then it really doesn't make any difference. I can notice that I'm not feeling too good, but if I don't get help, it means nothing. What is needed is to have an open discussion with family and friends. Too often, our discussions are all around logistics. "Hi, honey, how was your day?" "It was all right." "What did you do?" "Nothing." "Listen, do me a favor. Will you pick up the kids on the way home?" When it comes to actually talking about how we are feeling or what's really going on in our lives, we shy away from a discussion. That's true at home, and it's true at work. In truth, we need to open an honest discussion with our family and our officers. We need to be brave enough to ask, "Can I talk to you about something?"

Phase 2: Mild Symptoms

So, what if you ignore the warning signs outlined in Phase 1? The rust spot may have gotten bigger, but fortunately there is still time to take action.

Now you need to pay attention to these 10 symptoms:

1. Frequent loss of emotional control
2. Sleep disturbances/worrying
3. More frequent headaches, colds, stomach problems
4. Muscle aches
5. Intensified physical and emotional fatigue
6. Withdrawal from contact with others
7. Irritability
8. Intensifying depression/reduced concentration
9. Forgetfulness
10. Loss of sense of humor

Let's start with *frequent loss of emotional control*. Life at the Weaver house was often not very pretty. Just listen to a typical conversation – make that a rant—with my daughters and wife. "You know something? If I have to come home one more time to a toy on the stairs, somebody's going to get it. Now, come down here and pick this up. I can't believe these kids. They never listen to me." Does that sound familiar? Can you hear the crying going on while I was shouting? For many officers, this is "normal" life in their homes because they feel like they have lost control, and always sound angry. I didn't recognize myself anymore as a spouse or a parent. I was filled with constant regret that I was failing my kids, but couldn't seem to be able to stop my behavior.

I cannot tell you how many wives have come to me and asked, "Would you please tell my husband to stop yelling at the kids all the time?" Sometimes, we even develop strategies that make us believe that our behavior is not hurting our children. One officer came up to me after I relayed the story about yelling at my kids about toys on the stairs. He said to me, "You know, I just yelled at my kid about the same thing the other day and I actually threw the toy across the room. But it's okay, because every time I do that, I make sure I go and buy my son another toy." I just looked at him and said, "Man, your son doesn't need another toy. He just needs for his dad not to do that anymore."

Sleep disturbances and *worrying* are also symptoms of cumulative stress. Many of us in law enforcement are constant worriers filled with concern about the "what ifs." We toss and turn over the possibilities and our "what if" thinking takes on a life of its own. There was a study that found that over 90% of all the stuff that we worry about and causes us to become sick, get ulcers, and lose sleep, never happens. Chances are that the 10% or less that we worry about will happen regardless if we are worrying.[2] Worrying is like rocking in a rocking chair; it will give you something to do, but it's not going to get you anywhere. If we start worrying excessively to the point where it is interfering with our lives, it may be a symptom of cumulative stress. If we are constantly having a hard time falling asleep, staying asleep, or sleeping too much because of worry, then it is time to take some kind of action. Yes, all of us have an occasional sleepless night because something is on our mind, but if this becomes routine behavior for you, then it is time to seek help.

The third, fourth and fifth symptoms of cumulative stress show themselves primarily in physical ways: *more frequent headaches, colds, and stomach problems*; *muscle aches*; and *intensified physical and emotional fatigue*. Then, you may find yourself withdrawing from contact with others. This isn't simply about wanting some alone time; it's about not wanting to be around anybody. When I was suffering from cumulative stress, I just wanted to be left alone and not hang out with anyone, even my closest friends. *Isolation* and *withdrawal from people* are major indicators of suicidal thoughts, which I quickly found out. Now add on *irritability, intensified depression, lack of concentration*, and *forgetfulness*. Again, I am not talking about feelings that may be caused by a specific situation or even age. Instead, these are emotions and reactions that are not a normal part of your personality. They are symptoms that indicate a change in your psyche, just like a fever, sniffles, or cough may indicate you have the flu or a cold.

The final symptom is one that we also talked about as a warning sign – *loss of sense of humor*. Multiple studies have shown the importance of humor to moderate stress at work and during general life situations. In the case of cumulative stress, however, humor may take a dark turn like gallows humor. We find ourselves laughing at things that aren't really funny in real life. We believe it is a coping mechanism, but it is really avoidance to seek out the help we need. We think it makes us feel better, but instead the rust spot just keeps growing. Loss of a sense of humor, along with these other symptoms in Phase 2, indicates that the problem is not going to go away on its own. We can't ignore or disregard the signs or symptoms. Instead, intervention requires an aggressive lifestyle change that balances work and home life and allows us to develop strategies to reduce stress in every aspect of our life. Often, short-term professional counseling is also helpful.

Phase 3: Entrenched Cumulative Stress Reaction

At this phase, if you haven't sought help during phases 1 and 2, then you are now dealing with a lot of rust on your car. Your reaction to cumulative stress has become entrenched and is impacting your life. These are almost two dozen reactions you may see. Some of these reactions like loss of concentration, irritability, anger, and migraine headaches are the same as in phase 2 but more intense. Others are different and encompass physical, emotional and psychological aspects of people's lives.

1. Skin rashes

2. General physical and emotional fatigue

3. Intense depression

4. Increased alcohol use

5. Use of non-prescription drugs or illicit use of prescription drugs

6. Increased smoking

7. Elevated blood pressure

8. Crying spells

9. Intense anxiety

10. Cardiac problems

11. Rigid thinking

12. Withdrawal from friends, family, coworkers

13. Restlessness

14. Insomnia

15. Loss of concentration and attention span

16. Migraine headaches

17. Poor/increased appetite

18. Loss of sexual drive

19. Ulcers

20. Intense irritability/anger

21. Marital discord and relationship problems

As you read on, you'll see that I've dedicated entire chapters in this book on addiction and family issues. As I examine addiction in more detail later, it is important to note that 19% of law enforcement officers have a substance use disorder—not just a beer every once a while, but a diagnosable disorder[3].

Alcohol and suicide go hand-in-hand with 40 percent of suicides involving alcohol use.[4] When you recognize yourself, your family members, or your officers drinking more than usual, it is an indicator of something. Law enforcement officers self-medicate a lot of their stuff with alcohol and with drugs. Does anybody think that the use of drugs in policing doesn't happen? We self-medicate the exact same way other people self-medicate because we're people. Unfortunately, it has a whole different side effect on our careers.

Because we haven't dealt with cumulative stress in Phases 1 and 2, the effect it is having on us is solidifying—increased smoking, elevated blood pressure, crying spells, and cardiac problems. We are all different so our reaction to stress is different. But what is common among us is that the rust spot is no longer cosmetic; it is spreading to the very structure of the car and threatening its integrity as a drivable vehicle. Life is getting tougher and more painful. Now it is necessary to seek help from a health care provider as our reactions become entrenched in our life.

Phase 4: Severe Debilitating Cumulative Stress Reaction

The list of reactions to cumulative stress in Phase 4 is daunting. More importantly, the reactions are severe and debilitating to your life. In fact, they may end your life. If you are experiencing any of these reactions, you need to seek professional help immediately. These reactions will not go away. You may need therapy and/or even medication. Minimally, you need to talk to someone who has the extensive training required to help you. Here are reactions for you to be aware of in yourself and others. I will mention and examine a majority of them in the chapter on suicide because that's how daunting they can be:

1. Severe emotional depression (hopelessness, helplessness, worthlessness)

2. Lowered self-esteem

3. Lowered self-confidence

4. Inability to perform one's job

5. Inability to manage one's personal life

6. Severe withdrawal

7. Asthma, heart disease, diabetes, cancer

8. Uncontrolled emotions; anger, grief, rage

9. Suicidal or homicidal thinking

10. Life threatening/reckless behavior

11. Feelings of being expendable

12. Giving away possessions

13. Extreme chronic fatigue/ muscle tremors

14. Over reaction to minor events

15. Agitation

16. Poor concentration and attention span

17. Frequent accidents

18. Carelessness

19. Forgetfulness

20. Feelings of hostility

21. Intense feelings of paranoia

22. Moderate to severe thought disorder

23. Self-Injury

I'd like to spend a little time on *self-injury*. Self-injury is done by people of all ages, unlike the common perception that self-injury is just a teenage girl or boy thing, and only involves cutting, burning, or other physical injuries that we can see. Self-injury itself is not a mental illness, but a symptom of an underlying mental health issue. It's often associated with the belief and feeling that physical pain will alleviate emotional pain. It's a coping mechanism, albeit not a healthy one, that helps an individual deal with a variety of challenges.

For example, I once had a person in one of my classes share with me that they had tremendous emotional trauma and abuse as a child. One thing she did to cope was to run marathons. These marathons weren't your typical 26-mile ones, but the extreme 50-100-mile marathons. These marathons created incredible physical demands on her body, but she admittedly did them to self-medicate the pain that she was experiencing from childhood. After her husband who she ran with died by suicide, the pain increased, and she began running even more as a way of punishing herself for not having been able to stop him.

I could spend an entire chapter on self-injury, but please know that it can and is done by anyone and comes in a variety of forms, not always just cutting, burning, or things you can see. If you, or someone you know or love, are engaging in self-injury of any type, professional help is vital to not only find new and positive coping skills, but more importantly understand the 'why' that is causing this behavior in their life.

People are Different

For any of the four phases listed, it's important to remember that all of us respond to stress in different ways. Many people have asked how many signs or symptoms a person needs to have before there is concern. Like anything else, it all depends on the person. Not everyone who gives away possessions is suicidal. Not everyone who has low self-esteem or anger is at risk of cumulative stress. It's most commonly a combination of signs and symptoms—both internal and external—that determines where a person is at. Some of what has been listed in this chapter are mild warning signs, and some can be life-threatening. Simply letting the rust go and allowing it to take over our car, or spray painting over it and pretending it's not really there, can and will create havoc in our lives, both personally and professionally. Taking care of our rust spots early can help save our careers, our families, and possibly even our life.

CHAPTER 10

THE PAIN OF PTSD

Even though I retired from the police department in 2005, I wasn't diagnosed with post-traumatic stress disorder (PTSD) until many years later when the flashbacks, dark memories, nightmares, and additional suicidal thoughts started happening. My years in law enforcement had caught up with me. By the time of my diagnosis, I had spent significant time learning about and teaching mental illness. I have to admit it took me by surprise that I had PTSD. Much of what I had been diagnosed with and treated for in the past, such as major depression and anxiety, were actually part of my PTSD. For the first five years after I retired, I had no symptoms or simply didn't recognize them as symptoms. I, like many people, didn't realize that PTSD could go and come at different times in your life. You can experience symptoms of PTSD, then be relatively okay for a while, and experience the symptoms all over again.

There are a lot of misconceptions about PTSD, and we are learning more and more all the time. For years, it had been only really associated with war. In the Civil War it was called "Soldier's Heart," in WWI it was called "Shell Shock," in WWII it was referred to as "War Neurosis," and during Vietnam, it was labeled as "Combat Fatigue." It wasn't until 1980 that it became known as Post Traumatic Stress Disorder.[1]

We know now that PTSD can affect anyone—children and adults—exposed to trauma; sexual assault, a major motor vehicle accident, a major weather event, being present when a loved one is killed, exposure to long-term abuse, and so many other events can lead to PTSD. The list could be endless. Trauma is personal to the individual. Everyone deals with trauma differently. Not all trauma is the same. One incorrect assumption that I can't emphasize enough is that you need to be exposed to actual trauma to be diagnosed with PTSD. That is not true. Witnessing trauma also can lead to PTSD. As I mentioned earlier regarding vicarious trauma, we know that many people who watched 9/11 unfold on television suffered the effects of PTSD. What we do know is that whether you are exposed or witnessing, you are dealing with events that overwhelm your problem-solving and coping mechanisms and capabilities. The events are beyond what you know how to deal with, experience or understand.

Another misconception is that PTSD symptoms only occur directly after a traumatic event. While symptoms can show themselves immediately, sometimes they may not show up for months or years. For example, you can't stop thinking about the event, are still having trouble sleeping, or are having difficulty with relationships – months or years after the event occurred. A final misconception is that you can self-diagnose PTSD. Most people will feel anxiety or stress after experiencing or witnessing a traumatic event. That's called being human. PTSD is different and needs to be diagnosed by a professional. PTSD affects 3.6% of the U.S. adult population—about nine million individuals. About 37% of those diagnosed with PTSD are classified as having severe symptoms. Although men are more likely to experience traumatic stress, women are significantly more likely to experience PTSD[2]. Added stress can make someone more prone to PTSD, while having more social and familial support actually can cause it to be less debilitating. However, we also know that while stress can be a trigger, Adverse Childhood

Experiences (ACE), the traumas that many of us faced and were exposed to as children, are often the culprit for individuals who develop PTSD.

So, let's be very specific about defining this mental illness. Trauma is a highly individualized experience. PTSD evolves from an event that a person witnesses, experiences and/or is directly involved that the individual perceives as a threat to their safety. Therefore, an incident that I may witness, experience or be involved in that causes PTSD, e.g: a car accident, may not cause the same traumatic stress experience for my passenger who experienced the same car accident. PTSD is a serious condition that needs to be diagnosed and treated by a trained medical or mental health professional.

PTSD Symptoms

U.S. Department of Veteran's Affairs National Center for PTSD provides four types of PTSD symptoms[3], which may not be exactly the same for everyone.

1. **Reliving the event (also called re-experiencing symptoms).** Memories of the traumatic event can come back at any time. You may feel the same fear and horror you did when the event took place. For example:

   - You may have nightmares.

   - You may feel like you are going through the event again. This is called a flashback.

   - You may see, hear, or smell something that causes you to relive the event. This is called a trigger. News reports, seeing an accident, or hearing a car backfire are examples of triggers.

2. **Avoiding situations that remind you of the event.** You may try to avoid situations or people that trigger

memories of the traumatic event. You may even avoid talking or thinking about the event. For example:

- You may avoid crowds, because they unpredictable and therefore, feel dangerous.

- You may avoid driving if you were in a car accident or if your military convoy was bombed.

- If you were in an earthquake, you may avoid watching movies about earthquakes or traveling to areas that have a high rate of earthquakes.

- You may keep very busy or avoid seeking help because it keeps you from having to think or talk about the event.

3. **Negative changes in beliefs and feelings.** The way you think about yourself and others changes because of the trauma, which has many aspects, including the following:

- You may not have positive or loving feelings toward other people, and may stay away from relationships believing that it is easier to isolate rather than tolerate the unpredictability and emotional stressors of relationships.

- You may forget about parts of the traumatic event, or not be able to talk about them.

- You may think the world is completely dangerous, and no one can be trusted.

4. **Feeling keyed up (also called hyperarousal).** You may be jittery, or always alert and on the lookout for danger. You may often feel irritable and may have sudden bursts of anger that far exceeds the triggering incident. This is known as hyperarousal. For example:

- You may have a hard time sleeping.

- You may have trouble concentrating.

- You may be startled by a loud noise or surprise.

- You might want to have your back to a wall in a restaurant or waiting room.

Let's talk about a few of these symptoms, based on my own experiences and discussions with hundreds of other people during my classes across the country. I have difficulty falling and staying asleep. I realize that I don't want to go to bed because I know what the night is going to be like. It's been 15 years since I've retired, yet there are not many nights that I don't have a police-related dream. One of my recurring nightmares, which other officers have also shared with me, involves a shooting situation, even though I never fired my weapon in my career. In my nightmare, I have winter gloves on, and they are too big. I either can't get my gun out of my holster, or I can't pull the trigger. Over and over, night after night it plays out like that, leaving me very troubled. One of the things that I've recognized recently is that my dreams are now being acted out. I'm punching, kicking, and even grabbing my wife's hair while she is sleeping. I am sleeping through fights that I had as an active police officer.

The flashbacks are different. We often think of a flashback as something like what happens in a movie, like those times where a character goes back and recalls his childhood for 20 minutes. Flashbacks, literally those flashes of time which often only last seconds, are more than a memory; it feels like I am right back in the situation. I start to relive what happened and maybe, but not always, remember the details. I have flashbacks of my first trauma when I was 20 years old with the young man hanging in the jail cell, trying to revive a child who I knew was dead as her mother stood next to me screaming, and hearing the last breath of a woman in a car accident as I did my first compression. These images often reoccur without actively even thinking about the event. Suddenly, I'll be watching an episode of Seinfeld on television and an image from a traumatic event will just show up in my mind for no apparent reason.

Sometimes, I will have intense distress because of reminders of the trauma. It might be a movie, driving through a neighborhood, or seeing someone at Wal-Mart. I can experience a flashback where I am just feeling the fear, or pain, or whatever, in my body. My adrenaline and blood pressure will rise, and other physical reactions can occur like a pounding heart and increased anxiety.

Quite often, people with PTSD will have a diminished interest in activities. You don't want to go to a game, visit your relatives, or be involved in things that gave you joy. You may feel detached from others – isolated and withdrawn. You can't plan or think about the future because you are continually thinking about the trauma. You may also experience numbness and appear and/ or feel inclined to avoid people, places, or things that may trigger the feelings of trauma. I, like others with this disorder, even when I was working in Rochester, would avoid going down certain streets unless I had to. Some officers avoid driving by a certain house or location. You also avoid people who remind you of the trauma. I do that often. It causes you to isolate, even among fellow officers. You become withdrawn. You stop hanging out with people and having fun. This isolation, as we have discussed, can also be a sign and symptom of suicide.

Efforts to avoid feelings or triggers is one of the topics that officers relate to strongly when I am training. I am very honest and open with them about my own experiences. For example, I cannot go into the city of Rochester. I can drive around it, but I cannot drive through it because so much of my trauma occurred throughout the city. My reaction limits me at times. Once I was assigned to teach and certify instructors in Mental Health First Aid. At first, the training was assigned to a location outside of the city, but at the last moment it got moved to a building 100 feet away from one of my old section offices. Even though I wanted to do the week-long training and could have used the money, I had to cancel for my own mental health. My anxiety at the thought of driving to and being at that location for five straight days was debilitating. Canceling the training and not putting myself in the position of anxiety caused an incredible and deep sense of relief.

Several years ago, my wife and my granddaughter went out shopping, and I was taking a well-deserved nap on a couch. When my three-year-old granddaughter came home, she thought it would be funny if she climbed up on the end of the couch and dive-bombed her grandfather so he would wake up. She did exactly that, landing hard on my stomach, and immediately started laughing. I, on the other hand, was startled awake, and out of absolutely nowhere, started crying, "Please don't make me go to Rochester. Please don't make me go to Rochester. I can't go to Rochester. Please don't make me go." Now, keep in mind I wasn't dreaming about Rochester, law enforcement, or any specific events. Yet my immediate reaction of begging my wife in tears not to make me go to Rochester was really quite a telltale sign of the severity of my PTSD.

With PTSD, we often are unable to recall an important aspect of the trauma. That's an important thing for officers, departments, and the courts to know. Everyone reacts to trauma differently; the inability to recall important aspects of trauma can vary from person to person. You know that if you ask three people what they saw in a motor vehicle accident, quite often you get three different responses. That simply may mean that they have different perspectives and recollections of important aspects of the trauma. I often remind fellow officers and investigators that we have to recognize people's different aspects of experiencing a trauma. Even though you might have witnesses or officers tell different versions of an incident that involves some kind of trauma, it does not mean that they're not being truthful. They just simply had different recollections of how it happened. That's what trauma does to us. Trauma doesn't necessarily mean that everyone sees or recognizes the same thing in precisely the same way.

One aspect of PTSD that can be very troubling is the outbursts of anger and irritability. It was a real eye-opener for me when I realized that my yelling and taking out my anger on people was not simply part of my depression; it was all part of my PTSD. I also had difficulty concentrating and understanding what people were saying. I knew it wasn't age-related, but rather the distraction of all these flashbacks and memories as well as lack of sleep. I also experienced increased vigilance where I saw a bad guy on every corner and believed everyone was out to get my family and me. That increased vigilance meant that I – like many cops – didn't sit with my back to an open door in a restaurant. When increased vigilance becomes maladaptive, it can cause problems in our lives and relationships. I also still experience an exaggerated startle response with PTSD, where the slightest little thing startles me. I admit that I'm the first one to jump during a scary movie.

Some of the symptoms I have just described don't necessarily mean you have PTSD. Even if you had experienced or viewed a traumatic event, you can be dealing with Post-Traumatic Stress, but **not** PTS *Disorder*. You may experience some symptoms and then they go away. You may find healthy coping mechanisms to recover from a trauma. You may attend a crisis or stress management program or talk with friends, family, or a counselor. You may eat nutritiously or exercise more regularly, but not in a way that is isolating you or causing you to self-medicate. You may throw yourself into work. Long-term trauma can interfere with healthy development and affect a person's ability to trust others, manage emotions, navigate and adjust to life changes, and can threaten our very sense of personal safety.

But do not underestimate PTSD. For years, I was misdiagnosed, and it took a heavy toll on me. PTSD is a vastly under diagnosed disorder within law enforcement and corrections. As I mentioned, PTSD was initially known as shell shock or battle fatigue syndrome. War veterans first brought PTSD to the attention of the medical community, but as we become more aware of the pervasive effects of trauma on a person's life span, we know now and are constantly still learning that PTSD can occur in anyone who has experienced a traumatic event that threatens their safety, or involves death or violence. As I teach in my CIT classes, PTSD can also be seen in the people we deal with every day, including crime victims, inmates, and people we arrest. The truth of the matter is that in our very intense and violent world, PTSD is not confined to the battlefield. Our battlefield is played out today on the streets, in hospitals, in jails, and for some, simply in life in their own homes.

Recovering from PTSD

The first thing someone needs to do, if you, your loved ones or colleagues suspect PTSD is an issue, is to have it diagnosed by a professional through an actual psychological evaluation. This is a complex disorder that needs the correct diagnosis and treatment. Gaining a deep understanding of what PTSD or any other mental illness you or a loved one is dealing with is, is called psychoeducation; learning to understand your disorder. As we look at the number of people dying by suicide, with substance abuse disorders, experiencing domestic violence, getting divorced, and having heart problems, so many of those issues involve PTSD. Like others, I needed to recognize that I was not alone. One of the greatest benefits of that is realizing that there are other officers experiencing the same thing. We are not alone in our struggles. We have family members, friends, and critical incident stress management teams to help us. We have commanders and supervisors to help us. We have mental health agencies such as NAMI, the National Alliance on Mental Illness, mental health associations, specific police stress management organizations, and even trauma disorder centers, like the one that I was admitted to back in 2017 in Baltimore.

Even if you are displaying symptoms, PTSD is generally not diagnosed until at least one month after a traumatic event has occurred. At that point, a doctor will rule out physical illnesses as the cause of symptoms through a medical history and physical exam. There are no specific lab tests to diagnose PTSD; a psychiatrist, psychologist, or other mental health professional will usually employ an assessment tool to determine if you have PTSD. Assessment tools are simply a bunch of questions asked by a professional to make a determination and diagnosis of the illness. The problem, as has been discussed, is getting people in the door to take the assessment in the first place.

Treatment is focused on reducing emotional and physical symptoms, and may involve psychotherapy, medication, or both. The goal is to improve daily functioning, and help cope with the event that triggered the disorder. Recovery from PTSD is a gradual and ongoing process. While symptoms rarely go away completely, they can become less frequent and intense. In my own case, I have to be constantly vigilant about my mental health and work closely with my medical team relating to current and new treatments, including my most recent and successful treatment, ketamine infusion therapy.

Resilience

Often described as the ability to 'bounce back', it is one reason why many officers are able to go through their entire careers and not live with the issues of cumulative stress or PTSD. Many go through traumatic incidents and actually learn and grow from them, and they don't affect their ability to function. However, in no way, shape, or form does that mean that one officer is 'tougher' than another, which would imply that officers who experience serious effects of trauma are 'weaker'. Some officers are simply more resilient. As I have mentioned more than once, all of us are different. I may be more resilient in one area, and less resilient in another. Our resiliency depends on so many factors, including healthy coping mechanisms and positive social supports.

Here is perhaps the most important piece of information in this whole chapter. *There is increased research that says that early intervention with people who have suffered trauma can reduce the symptoms of PTSD and even prevent it altogether*[4]. I was not fortunate to live in a time when this point of view was even considered feasible. Today we have the ability to help so many by prevention and intervention. It's time we actually begin to implement it, not just in certain jurisdictions or in big departments, but with every law enforcement agency all around the country.

CHAPTER 11

OVERCOMING ADDICTION AND COMPULSIVE BEHAVIOR

I am not an expert on addiction and compulsive behavior, but as a police sergeant and pastor, I have lived and seen first-hand how addiction and compulsive behaviors can destroy individuals, families and relationships. I have also sought the advice of experts on this topic while writing this book.

Like many people at risk for addictive behavior, my journey started very young. As a child, I grew up with a stepfather who was an angry alcoholic. I had my first drink at age nine at a bowling alley, when he gave me an aspirin chased down with beer after I complained of a headache. My biological father introduced me to whiskey sours and hardcore pornography when I was 12. It didn't seem like a big deal to me that every time I visited him, I would have a drink and look at porn. At 14, I began to have sex.

I didn't really start to drink until I was 20, two years over the legal limit at the time. That was the same year I entered law enforcement. As cops, the term we sometimes use for drinking sessions is "choir practice," when we would gather after work and on our days off. I participated in choir practice at every possible time during the day – midnight, mornings and afternoons – and in many different locations—behind section offices, in parks, under bridges, and at strip clubs. We actually had a few bars and strip club owners open up for us at 8:00 a.m. to accommodate all of us who worked midnights. Other than officers, our choir practices consisted of some dispatchers and EMS folks. While it is sad and embarrassing to admit, I did drive home drunk on occasion and witnessed the same among fellow officers. I am eternally grateful that I never hurt anyone. And by the way, I know of other professions that do the same thing.

Problematic Behavior, Compulsion or Addiction?

During those years, I would usually only drink with other officers and rarely drank at home. Was I an alcoholic? My answer would be 'no'. Getting drunk with your colleagues from work once in a while or having a beer or glass of wine every day does not mean that you are an alcoholic. I did not fit into this definition of addiction: "a compulsive, chronic, physiological or psychological need for a habit-forming substance, behavior, or activity having harmful physical, psychological, or social effects and typically causing well-defined symptoms (such as anxiety, irritability, tremors, or nausea) upon withdrawal or abstinence."[1] There are many criteria for diagnosing a person's dependence on a substance, and a professional should always evaluate them.

I will say, however, that I definitely self-medicated with alcohol, sex, porn, and excessive exercise as I mentioned in the beginning chapters. Self-medication is the use of unhealthy coping strategies or activities to "feel better" and "to escape" the reality of our lives. Some people self-medicate depression with food, other self-medicate low self-esteem with sex, and still others try to escape financial problems with gambling. The list goes on and on. It can certainly become complicated. Self-medication doesn't have to be all bad. For example, sex between two people who care for one another is meant to be healthy and enjoyable, and we need food to survive. Using healthy coping skills such as exercise, or painting to manage emotions is also technically self-medication.

However, I also engaged in compulsive behavior—repetitive behaviors with no rational motivation that are often engaged in to reduce anxiety and are not necessarily considered a diagnosed condition[2]. Self-medicating, compulsive and addictive behaviors all involve a lack of control. Let's make it simple. Problematic behaviors refer to overdoing those behaviors. Compulsive behavior means that someone is losing control over those behaviors, and addiction refers to someone having no control over those behaviors.

Addiction in Law Enforcement

Addiction within the law enforcement community across America is a widespread and serious problem. One out of four police officers on the street has an alcohol or substance use issue, and substance use disorders among police officers are estimated to range between 20% and 30% as compared to under 10% in the general population[3]. A "red flag" or warning sign is that someone is changing over from "abuse" to "dependence" would be drinking more, taking more of a substance, or engaging in compulsive behaviors more and more to achieve the same results can be problematic.

Actual Substance Use Disorders, which often accompany or co-occur with depression/anxiety, PTSD or other high stress or trauma-related disorders, often hit law enforcement officers harder than many other professions. So why is addiction and compulsive behavior a bigger issue within law enforcement than other professions? Officers in treatment and/or recovery often report attempting to self-medicate depression or trauma with alcohol or other mood-altering substances as they openly discuss their addictions. In my view, it is because law enforcement officers are continually involved with other people's crises - stabbings, shootings, domestic problems, gang fights, homicides, civil unrest, and many others. These situations often involve life-threatening situations for the officer themselves. As has been discussed previously, these high stress situations—day after day and year after year—can cause a variety of responses and reactions. Making instantaneous decisions in high stress situations only adds to the stress level officers endure. Now add the fact that not everyone likes law enforcement. Being second-guessed by media, the community, and even our own departments can add a level of stress that many other occupations don't have. As I previously mentioned, on many occasions, children have given me the finger as their parents cheer them on. You don't see that happening to people in many other occupations. Now add the problems with the police culture and fear of getting help as I detailed earlier. Combine all of this, and it is not hard to understand why law enforcement may be more susceptible to addiction and compulsive behavior than many other professions.

Dr. Indra Cidambi, addiction expert and Medical Director at the Center for Network Therapy in New Jersey, states, "Repeated exposure to high-stress, life-threatening situations, coupled with long hours and an insular culture, appear to turn police officers toward alcohol or drugs in order to relax and cope. The good news is that they enter recovery faster when treatment integrates their living environment."

She continues, "Cops face high-stress situations several times a week, especially in urban areas. They are charged with making instant decisions in these immediate situations. To add to this pressure, of late, the whole community and sometimes the whole country judges them after the fact, while watching the news from the comfort of their homes, which adds a layer of guilt.[4]"

Let's take a more in-depth look at specific addictions and compulsive behaviors that affect law enforcement and the general population.

Alcohol

Alcohol addiction, also known as alcoholism, is considered a substance use disorder and reflects a person's inability to stop drinking, even when it causes extreme disruption in a person's life professionally, socially, and personally. Signs of alcohol addiction include frequently drinking more than intended, such as planning to just have 'one or two' drinks but actually having 12, being unable to drink more and more without becoming intoxicated, feeling symptoms of withdrawal when stopping, and spending an extreme amount of time trying to get and drink alcohol. A subset of problem drinkers is binge drinkers. These are individuals who consume excessive amounts of alcohol over a two-hour period. This is the category that I fell into. An infrequent binge drinker may be able to stop on his or her own. In many cases, prolonged binge drinking can develop into alcoholism.

People often say that they drink to "feel better," which is exactly the opposite of what it can do since alcohol is a depressant. You and I may be happy drunks for a couple hours, but then what happens? We crash. So, what do we do to remedy that? We drink more. If this cycle continues long and often enough, a person can begin to become addicted to alcohol. People who drink excessively (*key word*) aren't usually the ones who are whooping around dancing on tables. They may be the ones who are sitting at home on the back deck with seven or eight beers, or in front of the television with four or five glasses of wine. Those individuals are usually not drinking to "feel better'; they are quite often drinking so they don't feel at all. Though many view substance use, especially alcohol, as a normal way to manage stress, anxiety, and trauma, few expect it to grow into a problem of its own and rarely foresee the difficulties and challenges it will have on careers and families. For example, according to the World Health Organization, alcohol addiction is linked to at least 60 types of diseases or injuries, including those caused by accidents[5]. Anyone living with alcoholism is on a destructive path and, as difficult as it may be, friends and family should do all they can to help them seek recovery.

Four interview questions often used by physicians employ the *mnemonic,* CAGE as a useful and easy tool to check for alcohol dependence. The questions are designed to be less obtrusive than directly asking someone if they have a problem with alcohol and focus on **C**utting down, **A**nnoyance by criticism, **G**uilty feeling, and **E**ye-openers. The questions are:

1. Have you ever felt you should cut down on your drinking?

2. Have people annoyed you by criticizing your drinking?

3. Have you ever felt bad or guilty about your drinking?

4. Have you ever had a drink first thing in the morning to steady your nerves or get rid of a hangover?

A "yes" answer to at least two of those questions may suggest that there may be an issue with alcohol that needs to be addressed. Asking yourself or loved ones these questions certainly doesn't diagnose a substance use disorder, but it can certainly raise a red flag that one's alcohol consumption may be a problem and you need professional diagnosis and treatment.

Other Drugs

In a 2015 survey, the Substance Abuse and Mental Health Services Administration (SAMHSA) found that 18.9 million Americans, aged 12 and older, misused prescription drugs in the past year. About one percent of Americans aged 12 and older had a prescription drug use disorder[6]. And, these numbers are increasing[7]. Just like people outside of our profession self-medicate with substances, officers do as well. We self-medicate the same way other people do because we're just people—people who have difficulties, struggles, and pain as well as all of the stress and trauma that goes along with our profession. People become addicted to drugs because they are usually effective in relieving pain and are often legal.

Whether an individual abuses street or pharmaceutical drugs, however, the dangers can be endless. Like alcohol addiction, many people won't even admit that they are addicted at all. One reason is that we have a stigma about drug users, much like we do around mental illness. We use terms like druggy, meth-head, crackhead, and junkie just like we use terms like crazy and schizo for those who are mentally ill. No one wants to be thought of in that way. Law enforcement may also be a profession where men and women are more vulnerable because on-the-job injuries are often part of the job. When we receive a prescription from our doctor for pain medication, quite often we may not be told, nor do we usually ask about the potential additional risks. Some people, including law enforcement officers, can become addicted to illicit recreational drugs such as readily available cocaine or heroin. That type of addiction creates tremendous problems for officers, both personally and professionally. Because it is not nearly as common as other types of substance use in law enforcement, I won't go into any type of detail on the issue. However, if you, or someone you know or love, are addicted to illicit recreational drugs in any form, please get professional help as soon as possible, as the repercussions to life, family, and career are devastating.

Remember, substance use disorder is an illness that can affect your brain and behavior, making it difficult to control your use of drugs. The old belief that many people can just "stop doing it" is just as unhelpful as saying to a person with depression to just "snap out of it and be happy." Let's take a look specifically at some commonly misused prescription medications. Research shows that some prescription drugs are certainly more addictive than others. Most addictive drugs affect your brain's reward system by flooding it with dopamine. Dopamine plays a role in how we feel pleasure, and results in a pleasurable "high" that can motivate you to take the drug again. Overtime, you might become dependent on the drug to feel "good" or "normal." You might also develop a tolerance to the drug that can push you to take larger doses.

Opioids: These are types of drugs that may produce a euphoric effect or having the feeling of being "high," and are commonly prescribed for pain. Such opioids can include Oxycodone, Codeine, Fentanyl, and Demerol.

Benzodiazepine and Non- Benzodiazepine Medications: These central nervous system (CNS) depressants are medicines that include sedatives, tranquilizers, and hypnotics. These drugs can slow brain activity, making them useful for treating anxiety, panic, acute stress reactions, and sleep disorders.

- Benzodiazepines include Xanax, Librium, Valium (diazepam), Ativan (lorazepam), and Klonopin (clonazepam) triazolam (Halcion), and estazolam (Prosom) These are often called tranquillizers and can have a calming effect.

- Non-Benzodiazepines are such drugs as zolpidem (Ambien), eszopiclone (Lunesta), and zaleplon (Sonata). Ambien and Lunesta are very commonly prescribed sleep aids. They were once easy to obtain. However, it is still easy to get a script from your doctor, which can possibly lead to abuse and dependency.

Barbiturates are used mostly to relieve pain such as opioids and are often used for medical conditions such as epilepsy or other seizure disorders, and are not often thought of something that can be abused. However, if abused, they can be dangerous.

Stimulants increase brain activity to help boost alertness and energy levels. Stimulants such as amphetamine (Adderall) are commonly known as "speed." It is a CNS stimulant and is often widely prescribed for children to treat attention deficit hyperactivity disorder (ADHD) and narcolepsy. Products that contain amphetamine are often misused for their energizing effects. For example, Adderall can change to having the "speed" effect in older kids, college students, and adults. Sleep-deprived people such as students, truck drivers, and shift workers like police officers often misuse it. According to a University of Michigan study, nine percent of college students reported misusing Adderall[8]. Similar to Adderall, Ritalin increases levels of dopamine in the brain, which helps improve attention. Like other stimulants, it can be habit-forming. One reason that Ritalin and other prescription stimulants are commonly misused is their availability. Teenagers, young adults in college, and even parents often have ready access to them.

The above list is certainly not exhaustive. There are certainly other types of pharmaceutical and non-pharmaceutical drugs (including caffeine and tobacco) that can be addictive. I have been or am still on several of them—Demerol, morphine, codeine, and fentanyl for severe knee injuries/surgery from foot chases, being assaulted, as well as for back injuries and surgery from bodybuilding. I still take benzodiazepines for anxiety. Fortunately, I have not gotten addicted to these drugs, although I did develop a dependence on non-benzodiazepines for sleep at one time. It was difficult, but I was eventually able to come off them.

The drugs mentioned, most of which are obtained legally with a prescription, can do as much harm as illicit drugs if abused or used inappropriately. Contrary to what we often believe, just because a doctor prescribes a drug doesn't always mean that it's good. Each of us reacts differently to different drugs. As previously mentioned, if you or someone you know or love is addicted to medication in any form, please get that person professional help as soon as possible.

Gambling Addiction

Gambling is one of the more dangerous addictive behaviors. People get addicted to gambling because they believe they will win large amounts of money within a matter of minutes. They see this as a way to escape reality. How many of us tell our families and ourselves what we would do if we won the lottery jackpot of $500 million? How many of us have stood in line or witnessed someone purchasing 100 scratch-offs at the local gas station? How many of us have been to a casino where oxygen is pumped in and the sound of winning is played over the speakers to make you believe you could be the next big winner? There's a reason why casinos give out free drinks. The more you drink, the more you gamble which leads to more and more gambling to obtain the thrill associated with a big cash payout.

Often, people start gambling as just something fun to do, and it can soon become an addiction before they know it. Like any other drug, no one wakes up and says, "I hope to get addicted to gambling today." The results of gambling addiction are often devastating. It can leave people homeless, in serious debt, bankrupt, and divorced. I have seen over the years, personally and professionally, people addicted in this way. Helping yourself or someone else recognize and understand the problem is challenging. It can be incredibly difficult, but with appropriate help such as support groups and accountability partners, I have also seen people recover fully from it.

Food Addiction

Abusive eating is a bigger problem in the world today than most people think. It is not uncommon for people, including many law enforcement officers, to use food as a stress reliever or as a means of comfort when they are depressed, stressed, or grieving. But like drugs and alcohol, it can take on a life of its own in the form of addiction. According to the Food Addiction Institute, "When we are talking about a specific food as potentially being a substance of abuse, we are saying that the body has become dependent on a particular food or eating behavior. The most common addictive foods are foods high in sugar, flour, fat, grains and salt, or some combination of these. The most common addictive eating behaviors are binging, purging and volume eating. Food addiction is a chronic and progressive disease characterized by our seeking of the foods, or food behaviors we are addicted to, eating/doing them compulsively and having a great deal of difficulty controlling these urges despite harmful consequences."9

Unlike alcohol and drugs, most people – including the medical community – don't understand why or how food addiction happens. That is changing as more scientific evidence becomes available about this complex disease. What we do know is that for food addicts – just like alcoholics or drug addicts – it is not simply about wanting it to go away. Food addiction affects the brain, and simply wanting to stop does not make it happen. Fortunately, there are treatments that are currently helping people understand what triggers food addiction and how to manage it. In addition to food addiction, there are several forms of eating disorders that can affect people today. The two most recognized are anorexia, which is characterized by an abnormally low body weight, an intense fear of gaining weight and a distorted perception of it, and bulimia, which is characterized by someone who may secretly binge and then purge, trying to get rid of the extra calories in an unhealthy way. Both of these are serious medical conditions and can be life-threatening. These conditions are difficult to treat and need trained professional therapists that specialize in these disorders.

One of the most challenging pieces surrounding food addiction and other eating disorders is that unlike with addiction to drugs or alcohol, where an individual works toward sobriety and not consuming such substances, we all need food for survival. The National Eating Disorders Association is a great resource for information.

Sex and Pornography

Generally, it is incredibly difficult for someone to come forward and discuss sexual or pornography-related compulsive behaviors because of embarrassment, guilt, and shame. When

I discuss them openly in classes, I watch officers as they laugh and giggle with one another, put their heads down, or look out the window. I can relate because these were two of my compulsive behaviors that I used the most as a way to self-medicate and to deal with my low self-esteem. I didn't necessarily have affairs because of the act of sex, but to boost my self-esteem. I would feel proud of myself that I "still had it" enough to get a woman to be with me. Here was the catch—it never worked for any length of time. After one affair, I did the same thing again as I tried to make myself feel better about who I was. Like any other type of negative coping skill, I thought it worked, right up until it didn't, then it would happen again.

Pornography was an easy way to escape life altogether; to put myself in another world where I could just be someone else and leave all my problems behind, even for 10 minutes. Of course, that feeling doesn't last for any length of time either. So, I would look at it again, then again, then again, and not be able to stop. In today's world, with the accessibility and anonymity of the Internet, it can become more and more of an issue. Pornography did not become a multi-billion-dollar industry because of my past compulsions, so I am clearly not unique in all of this. But I think I am unique in that I openly talk about it. Contrary to popular opinion, these behaviors are absolutely not just a problem for men, but for women as well for the exact same reason. They can occur in anyone from recruit to chief, construction worker to mayor, from rich to poor, from child to adult. Remember that I began looking at hard-core pornography at 12 and started having sex at 14. I didn't know the term, but I was self-medicating then too. Then it simply became a way of life.

The Diagnostic and Statistical Manual of Mental Disorders-V (DSM-5) does not list sex addiction as a diagnosable condition yet, but research indicates that there is a clear prevalence of adverse sexual behavior that is similar, in development, to a "chemical" addiction. Because compulsive sexual behavior doesn't have its own diagnostic category in the DSM-5, it may be diagnosed as a subcategory of another mental health condition such as an impulse control disorder or a behavioral addiction.

According to the Mayo Clinic, compulsive sexual behavior is sometimes called hypersexuality, hypersexuality disorder, or sexual addiction. It's an excessive preoccupation with sexual fantasies, urges, or behaviors that is difficult to control, causes you distress, or negatively affects your health, job, relationships, or other parts of your life[10].

Compulsive sexual behavior may involve a variety of commonly enjoyable sexual experiences. Examples include masturbation, cybersex, multiple sexual partners, use of pornography or paying for sex with prostitutes. When these sexual behaviors become a major focus in your life, are difficult to control, and are disruptive or harmful to you or others, they may be considered compulsive sexual behavior.

No matter what it's called or the exact nature of the behavior, untreated compulsive sexual behavior can damage your self-esteem, relationships, career, health, and other people. But with treatment and self-help, you can learn to manage compulsive sexual behavior.

The Mayo Clinic lists several signs and symptoms[11]:

- You have recurrent and intense sexual fantasies, urges and behaviors that take up a lot of your time, and feel as if they're beyond your control.

- You feel driven to do certain sexual behaviors, feel a release of the tension afterward, but also feel guilt or remorse.

- You've tried unsuccessfully to reduce or control your sexual fantasies, urges or behavior.

- You use compulsive sexual behavior as an escape from other problems, such as loneliness, depression, anxiety or stress.

- You continue to engage in sexual behaviors that have serious consequences, such as the potential for getting or giving someone else a sexually transmitted infection, the loss of important relationships, trouble at work, financial strain, or legal problems.

- You have trouble establishing and maintaining healthy and stable relationships.

I know firsthand how difficult it is to read, understand, and admit some or all of the above indicators. Like substance-use disorders, compulsive sexual behavior may be a sign that there is a problem. And just like alcohol or drugs, more intensive sexual content and stimulation are typically required over time in order to gain the same satisfaction or relief. I could do an entire chapter just on this issue and how deeply it can and does affect many of us in law enforcement, including how these same disorders can affect our children. Seek professional help and counseling if you or someone you love feels that you or they have lost control of yours or their sexual behavior, especially if the behavior causes problems for other people. Just like anything else, compulsive sexual behavior tends to escalate over time, so get help when you first recognize there may be a problem.

Shopping Addiction

Compulsive shopping or what has been labeled by some as "retail therapy" is an activity that is growing at an unprecedented rate. Between constant marketing, free next day delivery, credit card limit increases, and both on-line and in person stores, compulsive shopping is a genuine concern. Like gambling, this behavior can easily lead to divorce and bankruptcy. It is absolutely critical to know that contrary to public perception, this is not a compulsion that only affects women. Stereotypes describe women shopping for jewelry, clothes, and shoes. But what do men typically buy when they engage in this behavior? Guns, trucks, motorcycles and four-wheelers. Men might not go out and buy five pairs of shoes, but we can't help but get that brand-new F-150 that just came out. Every time I teach any class of first responders, the parking lot looks like a used truck dealership.

Self-medicating in this way is generally the same as other addictions or behavior. We think it will make us feel better. We buy a new shirt or outfit, and two days later we want another one. We buy a new gun, and we immediately start shopping for the next one. Like any other addictive behavior, that revolving door technique doesn't work. It's really important to note that like any other addiction, it's not necessarily what you're doing, but why you are doing it. If you want a new car because your current one is old or the lease ran out, fine. But if you're buying a car or anything else to feel better about yourself, it may be a concern you might want to address. If this describes you or someone you love, recognize it, discuss it openly, and seek professional help if necessary.

Work

Though many of us find it hard to believe, work can be highly addictive. Focusing too heavily on our careers can lead to problems with our marriages and relationships in general. Work addiction is particularly prevalent among people who are constantly looking for the approval of others, trying to avoid other issues, or just love to do their job. For some of us, it's simply easier to be at work than at home, so we work overtime or ask to be called in for a SWAT call-out or homicide investigation. Work addiction can lead to lack of sleep, improper nutrition, emotional and physical exhaustion, pressure, and stress that becomes extremely dangerous to you and those around you. As I've mentioned several times, maintaining some type of proper balance between personal life and professional is the only way to leading a healthy lifestyle.

How to Identify Addiction Symptoms

I could talk in depth about other addictions like excessive Internet or video game use. But I believe I have made my point that what may start as self-medicating behavior for both law enforcement officers and the general public, can become serious addiction problems. So how do you identify addiction symptoms? While there are no steadfast rules to identifying the behaviors of an individual that may be signs of addiction, most of them can be recognized by common signs and symptoms, and some common characteristics. As you recall, a sign is something you see, and a symptom is something the person is experiencing. Some of these addictions and behaviors may have signs and symptoms that are easy to recognize, and some not so much. *Healthline* provides some very basic ways to identify someone with an addiction or behavior disorder, as well as certain signs and symptoms to look for in a person's personality[12].

1. **Identifying the initial signs.** In the early stages, a person might not show telltale signs of a full-blown addiction. What looks like addiction could be an experimental phase or a form of stress management. But a real addiction, if left untreated, can develop into a debilitating habit or increased risk of illness. Some early stage clues include:

    - Experimentation.

    - Family history of addiction.

    - Being particularly drawn to an activity or substance.

    - Seeking out situations where the substance or activity is present.

    - Episodes of binging or loss of control with little to no feelings of remorse after.

2. **Look for changes in personality.** After a person moves past experimenting or the early phase of addiction, they'll likely exhibit major personality or behavior changes. You

may notice an increase in alienation over time. People with an addiction tend to surround themselves with others who encourage their habits. When confronted, they may make excuses and try to justify their behavior to you. These changes may be infrequent at first. Telltale signs include:

- A lack of interest in hobbies or activities that used to be important.

- Neglecting relationships or reacting negatively to those closest to them.

- Missing important obligations like work.

- Risk taking tendencies, especially to get drugs or continue certain behaviors.

- Ignoring the negative consequences of their actions.

- Distinct change in sleeping patterns that result in chronic fatigue.

- Increased secrecy, like lying about the amount of substance used or time spent.

Helping Others

I'd like to discuss some ways to help support a fellow officer or family member dealing with an addiction or certain behaviors. How the person is approached is critical, since many of us become defensive or even embarrassed when we are confronted about any negative behaviors. Here are some helpful hints from the National Council for Behavioral Health's Mental Health First Aid program[13]:

- **Use Appropriate "I" Statements.** The use of "I" statements when starting a conversation is important. Statements such as "I am concerned...." "I recognize...." or "I see that you're...." can at least get a conversation started. Saying something like, "I think you're a drunk" is indeed an "I" statement, but certainly not an appropriate one.

- **Honesty.** Having the courage to be honest with someone—not just call someone out on their unhealthy behavior—is hard but necessary. Recognizing and actually expecting push back and denial is important in your conversations with someone.

- **Meet Them Where They Are.** Often asking confrontational or challenging questions right off the bat doesn't help in having an open conversation. Meeting the person where they are at the time is very important.

- **Decide If You Are the Right Person.** Identify if you are the right person to be having this conversation. Sometimes if you are too close to the individual, such as being in a relationship or parent/child, you might not be in the best position to address these issues. Please know that it is ok. But just like asking about suicide, don't just ignore it because you're not the right person. Find someone else who can. If the addiction or behavior is life-threatening, professional help and intervention is needed immediately.

- **Avoid Passing Moral Judgment.** Labeling someone as a "bad person" or an "addict" does not help provide an open conversation. Telling a person all the things they've done wrong and lecturing them on their faults will simply build a wall.

- **Don't Join in The Person's Behavior.** Asking someone to meet you at a bar so you can talk to them about their drinking problem is a bit counterproductive.

- **Don't Beg Someone to Stop.** An individual with an addiction or behavior disorder needs to recognize their own need for help. Pleading with a friend or loved one may work temporarily, but recovery first has to happen because it's what they need for themselves, not only for someone else.

- **Don't Make Excuses for Their Behavior or Taking Over Their Responsibilities.** This is really easy to do. "My husband isn't here at the game today because he had a really hard night." "My wife doesn't feel well so I'm here to pick up the kids today." The only thing this does is not hold them accountable for their behavior.

- **Try Not to Feel Guilty or Responsible for Someone Else's Behavior.** Hearing things like "I drink because of you," "I go to work because I can't stand being around you," "It's all your fault" are statements made to simply deflect their behavior onto the person trying to help. A person dealing with an addiction may point the finger at you but they, not you, are responsible for their own behavior.

As I previously stated, one of the biggest stigmas regarding substance-use and behavior disorders is that it's a choice. There's a reason they are called addictions and disorders. Recovery rarely happens by someone simply saying, "Stop it." If you or a loved one are suffering from any of what has been discussed in this chapter or another addiction or behavior, know that help is available. Asking for help doesn't mean that you can't handle your life or that you can't change someone else's behavior on your own. Once again, these are called addictions and disorders for a reason. That's why there are professionals out there trained in dealing with these very difficult issues. If mental health issues are triggering the urge to drink, use drugs and causing other issues in your life, know that support is out there. Employee/officer assistance programs, alcohol and substance use programs, addiction centers, are 12-step programs (some of which can simply be done online) are available.

In our law enforcement culture, we know that trusting others is an issue and for many a real concern. I understand that completely. But it's your life, the life of fellow a officer, friend, loved one, or family member that matters most. Asking for help is not a sign of weakness, but rather a sign of courage. Examples of support can be found at:

Warriors Heart: 888-438-6616 (24 hour support)
www.warriorsheart.com/lawenforcement

American Addiction Centers: 888-407-7949
www.americanaddictioncenters.org/law-enforcement

The Recovery Village: 877-491-2751 www.therecoveryvillage.com

12step.org (on-line treatment): www.12step.org

National Eating Disorders Association:
www.nationaleatingdisorders.org/

Mental Health First Aid: https://www.mentalhealthfirstaid.org

CHAPTER 12

THE ULTIMATE CONSEQUENCE: SUICIDE

Suicide : The intentional taking of one's own life. It's estimated that approximately every 48 hours, a police officer dies by suicide, totaling well over 200 law enforcement deaths each year[1]. Annually, nearly three times as many officers die by suicide than are killed by felons, making suicide the number one killer in law enforcement[2].

Suicide is not only rampant among law enforcement. It is an American endemic. In 2018, there were over 48,000 suicides in the United States[3]. That is a suicide about every 11 minutes[4]. Suicide is currently the 10th leading cause of death in United States, and it ranks as the second leading cause of death for 15-34-year-olds[5]. Additionally, there are approximately 1.4 million suicide attempts (age 18 and up) each year as well[6].

The highest risk group for suicide? Middle-aged white men[7]. The second highest risk for suicide is elderly men over the age of 85, and the second leading cause of death in people between 10 and 34[8]. It is also the second leading cause of death among college students[9]. There are more suicides in the U.S. than homicides[10]. Firearms accounted for 24,432 suicides in 2018 (50.5%).[11]

When I first started teaching on suicide in 2003, there were about 30,000 annually[12]. While fatalities for physical diseases like heart attacks and cancer have been steadily decreasing, the number of deaths by suicide, which is often connected to mental illness, has risen sharply. The American Foundation for Suicide Prevention estimates that approximately 90% of those who die by suicide have a diagnosable mental health disorder at the time of their death; most commonly depression[13]. Quite simply, mental illnesses like depression and PTSD can be fatal. The fatality of mental illness is called suicide.

A little over 50% of all suicides involve a firearm[14]. Certainly, it makes sense to realize that having a firearm in a home can put someone vulnerable to suicide more at risk. Although most people keep guns in their home for protection, 86% of the gun-related deaths inside people's homes are the result of a suicide. In the homes without firearms, only 6 percent of the suicides used a firearm.[15] And what do cops have in their homes? Guns, sometimes lots of them. Additionally, according to the American Association of Suicidology, male whites account for nearly 70% of all suicides and account for a high percentage of suicide by firearm[16]. As I've mentioned previously, policing has historically been a male, white-dominated profession, and as stated, law enforcement officers typically have guns.

Suicide Effect on Others

Behind all of those statistics are real people, and real families left behind to deal with their loss. Most officers around the country are familiar with suicide. Most have responded to some type of suicide scene, whether at someone's house or a jail cell. And of course, many are familiar with suicide when it comes to fellow officers. Among officers, the percentage is much higher. I will often ask in my classes, "Outside of your professional role, outside of your role as a police officer, please raise your hand if you know somebody who has died by suicide." Without fail, and for years on end, about 80% of the room would raise their hand. We know that suicide impacts officers' lives outside of policing because we're just people too. Unfortunately, suicide is a reality among law enforcement because we know and see people dying every day.

The number of survivors of suicide loss in the U.S. is more than 5.4 million and statistically, suicide will touch at least 50% of us in any given year[17]. Those nearly 50,000 people who die each year from suicide will affect many people. Recent research suggests that for each death by suicide, 147 people are affected by it[18]. Those of you who have lost or known someone who has died by suicide are suicide loss survivors. A suicide loss survivor means suicide has impacted your life in some way whether it took place six months, a year or 20 years ago.

Suicidal Feelings

Many people at some time in their lives think about suicide. Most decide to live because the crisis passes or the thought fades. Others experiencing a suicidal crisis sometimes *perceive*—and that's a key word—that their situations are inescapable, and they feel that they have utterly lost control of their lives.

LivingWorks, a wonderful suicide prevention organization based out of Calgary, Alberta, Canada, in their trainings such as Applied Suicide Intervention Skills Training (ASIST), and Safe-Talk, estimate that one out of every twenty people have thoughts of suicide in any given two-week period—not in a year, but in two weeks[19]. How does that apply to law enforcement? If you have a department of 100 officers, statistically five of them have thought of suicide in the last two weeks; you have a minimum of 1 out of 20 having thoughts of suicide every two weeks. But it is actually worse than that. According to the National Alliance on Mental Illness and the CDC, nearly one in four police officers thinks of suicide at some point in their life.[20] Between 7% and

19% of police officers have symptoms of post-traumatic stress disorder, as compared to 3.5% in the general population. More police die by suicide than by homicide: the number of police suicides is nearly 3 times that of homicides [21].

Imagine that you are reading this book, and it is just you and me in a room with no one around to hear. And I ask you, "At any point in time in your life, have you ever thought of suicide?" Many of you would respond, "Yes. There was that time. There was that one day. There was that first break up. There was that first time I didn't get promoted. First time I lost that job when I was a kid." The truth is that many of us have had thoughts of suicide that last for a split-second and we react by thinking, "Oh my God, what was that? Why in the world would I think that? That's ridiculous. I'm not going to kill myself." For some people, thoughts of suicide linger a few days. The thoughts kind of hang out and float around because of a difficult situation we are going through. Then the crisis ends, and we move on. Given our circumstances, they may or may not return. Every one of us has felt sad before, and just like emotional pain, reality tells us that we will feel sad again. That's unfortunately a part of life.

For others, however, suicide is part of our mental illness. My own thoughts of suicide are often. I used to think of killing myself every day, and sometimes still do. It's not very often that you get to hear from someone like me – someone who has been hospitalized nine times over the last 24 years in a psychiatric hospital for being suicidal. But even though suicidal thoughts are common, it is absolutely critical for us to know that those thoughts don't have to be acted upon. If I can provide you with what a person may be experiencing, I may be able to provide you with the skills enough to be empathetic when talking with someone who is suicidal.

We know that sometimes people who have thoughts of suicide, attempt suicide, or actually die by suicide feel as though they can't stop the pain. What kind of pain are we talking about?

Have you ever had a toothache before? What would you give at the peak of that toothache to make that pain go away? Almost anything, right? In the case of suicide, even though it can certainly be actual physical pain, it is most often emotional pain. Every one of us has felt emotional pain before in our lives, and the reality is that every one of us will feel emotional pain again. That's part of life. Sometimes what happens for those who have thoughts of suicide is that the emotional pain becomes so great, that, like getting rid of your toothache, they can feel the only way to make the pain go away is to make themselves go away. They are unable to make decisions and are feeling trapped, hopeless, helpless, and worthless. Unfortunately, many also have a difficult time indicating these things to the people they love, and the people that love them back. For many, sadness can become a way of life, and sometimes people feel that they can't make the sadness go away. They think, "Even though it seems like I've got everything going for me, I can't take this feeling anymore."

As difficult as this might be to understand, individuals who die by suicide don't necessarily want to die. They simply sometimes don't want to live the way they're living. If given another choice, most often they would choose life. ASIST training describes that as suicidal ambivalence. Part of them does in fact want to die, but there's part that still wants to live. In most of us, our life side is stronger than our death side. For others, however, their death side takes over, and people take their life.

Fatal Myths

In our society we have created myths about suicide that can be fatal. Here are several that you should take note of:

Only certain types of people are at risk for suicide. Although there are groups of individuals who may be statistically at greater risk, having thoughts of suicide and actually dying by suicide happens regardless of socio-demographics and environmental factors. Individuals of all races, creeds, incomes, and educational levels die by suicide. There is no typical suicide victim, and anyone can be at risk for suicide.

Sometimes, a bad event can push people to kill themselves. The types of suicide in which someone just broke up with a girlfriend and then go kill themselves are rare. However, we do know that a single event may be "the last straw" in a series of events for the individual. There may be circumstances or events in a person's life that are more stressful than others, and everyone's coping abilities are different. Therefore, stressful events and a person's ability to cope with a stressful event are subjective.

Suicide is selfish. This belief is a common one among suicide loss survivors. "Why would they do that to their family?" "Didn't they know how horrible this would be for everyone?" Once again, it is important to remember that someone having thoughts of suicide is experiencing some kind of psychiatric crisis. What happens in a crisis is that thoughts become distorted. When I say, "My wife and my family would be better off without me," I truly believe in my distorted thinking that she and everyone else actually would be. After all, look at what I'm putting them all through, right?

During that distorted thinking, people believe that at that moment, the most selfish thing they could do is stay alive and keep their families in misery. They truly believe that the most *self-less* thing to do is to kill themselves, believing that life for their loved ones would be better and happier if they were gone. Is that a true statement? Would the family actually be happier? Absolutely not. The impact on families who lose loved ones to suicide is overwhelmingly tragic. If you ever believe that your family would be better off without you, it's simply not true—despite what your mind is telling you.

If I ask someone about suicide, it will give him or her the idea. This myth has existed for a very long time and has prevented thousands of people from asking someone about suicide. It's the myth that if you ask someone about suicide, you will put the thought of killing themselves in their head. This is simply not true. Asking someone about suicide does not give him/her the idea. If you have gotten to the point that a person's indicators and warning signs are leading you to ask that very important question, that person has more than likely thought of suicide well before you ask. Asking does not plant the seed of suicide in someone's mind that is not already thinking about it.

Instead, talking about suicide allows people to seek help and share their stories. It takes away the stigma. Can you imagine not talking about your broken leg because of how people would respond? Does not talking about birth control keep teenagers from getting pregnant? By treating suicide as a dirty secret and something that will spread if talked about, we give it power and take away important tools to help prevent fatalities.

The Language of Suicide

For so many people, suicide isn't really on our radar until we are touched by suicide in some way – either through the loss of a friend or loved one, someone we know experiencing suicidal thoughts, or our own suicidality. Most of us are unaware of the warning signs and often feel guilty because we didn't know at the time. We can, however, learn the language of suicide now.

Dr. Thomas Joiner has spent his career studying suicidal behavior. In a paper for the American Psychological Association, he discusses his interpersonal-psychological theory[22]:

The interpersonal-psychological theory of suicidal behavior proposes that an individual will not die by suicide unless he/she has both the desire to die by suicide and the ability to do so. What is the desire for suicide, and what are its constituent parts? What is the ability to die by suicide and in whom and how does it develop?

In answer to the first question of who desires suicide, the theory asserts that when people hold two specific psychological states in their minds simultaneously, and when they do so for long enough, they develop the desire for death. The two psychological states are perceived burdensomeness and a sense of low belongingness or social alienation.

In answer to the second question regarding capability for suicide, self-preservation is a powerful enough instinct that few can overcome it by force of will. The few who can have developed a fearlessness of pain, injury and death, which, according to the theory, they acquire through a process of repeatedly experiencing painful and otherwise provocative events. These experiences often include previous self-injury, but can also include other experiences, such as repeated accidental injuries; numerous physical fights; and occupations like physician and front-line soldier in which there's exposure to pain and injury, either directly or vicariously, is common.

When it comes to warning signs, there are a variety of ways that people can "talk" about suicide. Although it is difficult for people to acknowledge—especially those who have lost someone to suicide, the majority of people who die by suicide told someone along the way. But how do people talk about suicide? We know that not all our communication is verbal. Sometimes people talk about suicide through behaviors, attitudes, thoughts, or physical indicators.

Behavior as the Language of Suicide

Reckless behavior can put the individual at risk of harm or death. Reckless behavior can range from bungee jumping to driving while intoxicated. We also have heard about suicide by cop, when people become so lost and suicidal that they deliberately put themselves in a position to be killed by the police. It's a tragic situation for the person, and also a tragic and frustrating one for the officer involved and his/her family and department. But what about the other thing that nobody talks about—suicide by suspect?

I thought that if I could intentionally put myself in positions in which my life could be endangered (outside of normal everyday work), I would not only die but also go out a hero. So, I was the first to go into a house or kick in a door on a "man with a gun" call. I was the first to hide inches from a drug house door dressed in camouflage, knowing what would probably happen if I got caught. I was the first to pull someone out of a car door during a felony stop. Everyone thought I was just really tough; little did they know that I just wanted to die. I figured that if I got killed in the line of duty, I would get an awesome funeral with a flag over my coffin, someone would be playing taps, and I would be remembered, like I said, as a hero. And my wife would get double my life insurance.

Do you think I am the only cop that has ever thought that way? The answer is 'no'. I might be one of the only one that admits it, but I really don't think that I'm the only one who has ever thought it. The lesson in this is that if you find yourself doing these behaviors for that same reason, recognize what you're doing. Secondly, if you see fellow officers putting themselves at risk or in dangerous situations, don't simply assume that they're just tough guys who want to get the job done. They may, in fact, want to get their life over with. Whether you are a supervisor or fellow officer, *please* call them on their actions and ask them why they are doing what they are doing. It may help save a life.

Withdrawal from family, friends, school, work, or other social gatherings. I'm not simply talking about having some alone time. I'm talking about literally withdrawing from life. Many of us want to be alone after a bad day, but in reality, that's one of the worst things we can do. Withdrawing and isolating from others is an important behavior that should not be ignored or simply brushed off, thinking someone just needs their space.

Loss of interest in things normally enjoyed. Suddenly, your son doesn't want to play baseball anymore, your mom no longer wants to come over for dinner, or you start to care less about your favorite football team. The examples are endless. When someone starts to lose interest in things that once brought them joy, they are saying something.

Abuse of alcohol, drugs, or an increase in other self-medicating behaviors. Substance-use will be discussed later as just one self-medicating behavior. But an increase in any self-medicating behavior such as gambling, sex, and shopping or desperate feelings of wanting to escape from reality is a way that people may be talking to you about suicide.

Giving away possessions. Giving away possessions may be a huge indicator of someone having thoughts of suicide. Back in 1996, I had a Chevy Beretta. Anyone remember those cars? My red five-speed Beretta was awesome and fast with a sunroof and spoiler on the back. One day, I drove it to Sears and had an AM/FM cassette player installed. You can envision how long ago it was, right? My wife at the time was standing in the driveway when I got home. She asked me where I had been and I replied, "Honey, I just went and got a radio and new cassette player in my car," excitedly. She wanted to know why I chose the most expensive brand of radio when we didn't really have the money for it. My oldest daughter was turning 16 at the time and I explained to my wife, "The reason I got it is because when I kill myself, my daughter is going to get the car and I want to make sure she has a good radio in it." My wife just looked at me and sighed as I had said it so matter-of-factly. I wasn't sad, crying, or in any type of crisis. I just thought it was a nice thing to do. That's distorted thinking.

When suddenly you see family members, friends, or fellow officers giving important and personal stuff away, it can be indicator of something. Those with thoughts of suicide often want to make sure that their family is all set when they are gone, or that loved ones have what is important to them. Whether it's a car or giving away a pet to a family member or the humane society, the behavior is the same. That doesn't mean every time someone gives you something, that they are thinking of suicide. But if it's combined with other indicators, it could be something that needs to be addressed.

Extreme behavior changes. Certainly, it's understandable when we see someone go from a happy to a depressed state, that they may be going through some type of difficult time. What about the opposite? What about the person who's been down and out for the last couple of months, then comes to work happy and seemingly without a care in the world? That can be an indicator for suicide. When someone is depressed, it's often even too hard for people to have the energy to kill themselves. But when someone decides on suicide, they may begin to feel relieved or at peace, since they feel as though they have a solution.

When this happens, you may need to actually ask someone why he or she is so happy. It sounds kind of stupid but it's something that may need to be addressed. Common sense tells us that normally we would say, "Oh, thank goodness you're finally out of your little funk. You've been dragging all of us down. Glad you've snapped out of it." But that may be the exact opposite of what is needed. Instead, I recommend a different approach. "I know you've been pretty down lately; you've been going through a lot. But in the last couple of days you've been up and acting like yourself again. Can I ask you what may sound like a stupid question? Exactly, why are you so happy?" Believe it or not, the answer may lead to a discussion surrounding suicide.

Impulsivity. Alcohol or other drugs can often induce this behavior; we often don't act like ourselves when we are intoxicated. We say things we might not normally say and do things we might not normally do. One-third of suicides involve heavy use of alcohol before the attempt, according to a new study by researchers at the University of California, Los Angeles (UCLA)[23]. When we drink, our impulsivity increases. It increases whether or not you have a diagnosable mental health disorder. If you're already struggling with thoughts of suicide, adding alcohol and/or drug use to your life certainly won't make it better.

Making Amends. Making things right with someone they have hurt in the past or asking for forgiveness from someone they feel they have harmed in some way can be warning signs of suicide. Of course, this is one of the 12 steps in most 12 step programs, but outside of that, making amends can be a distinct warning sign that should at least be addressed.

Beliefs and Feelings as the Language of Suicide

Feelings of desperation or feelings of being trapped. I have experienced this more than almost any other feeling. "There's no way out of this" or "I've got to get out of here" expresses the deep desire to escape whatever situation you feel is inescapable. For most people, those moments come and go, and then come and go again. The problem arises when the feelings of desperation and being trapped become so incredibly powerful that rational thinking no longer exists. Abuse and acute financial stress can lead to feelings of extreme desperation, but for those with a mental illness, it can also be triggered in a second by something completely innocuous.

Not too long ago my wife, Lynne, and I were driving to Florida. We had put an offer down on a condo, and we were driving down to start the moving-in process. We were only going to be gone for about 10 days. This was a dream of ours—to have a place up in New York for the summer and a place in Florida for the winter. How could it get any better? Lynne was driving, and as we were around Virginia going about 70 mph, a horrific sense of desperation hit me after having a fight with one of my daughters on the phone. Suddenly, I felt trapped in my brain, not the car. Feelings and thoughts of suicide flooded my mind, I began to breakdown and cry, saying things like, "I can't do it" and "Please let me go."

We were in the passing lane and a tractor-trailer was directly next to us. As I sat in the passenger seat, I looked at the wheels of the trailer and started to take off my seat belt. I envisioned opening the door and jumping out into the path of the truck. I was crying and asking Lynne to just let me go. I was so scared, and as Lynne tried to talk and settle me down, my heart was pumping so fast that I thought for sure this was it. Then in this incredibly irrational state, the rational thought that I did not want my wife to witness my suicide came over me. I took my hand off my seatbelt and sat up...Crisis over. I have faced similar thoughts as I've driven through tunnels, up to on-coming trains, and a whole host of other things because of desperate and trapped feelings...Scary moments.

Anger and Rage. These are powerful emotions that can quickly become out of control because they are easy to express. When I was a pastor, I would do a lot of couple's counseling. So often couples would come in and one of them would talk about the other's extreme temper, and it wasn't too long into the session that our conversation would turn to the issue of depression.

That link between anger and depression reminds me of an article I was in, several years ago in *Reader's Digest*. The name of the article was *The Secret that Men Won't Admit*[24]...Catchy little title, right? I'm sure that lots of women sitting in the doctor's offices wondered what the big secret was that we'd been keeping from them for all these years. The whole point of that article was how depression in men primarily comes out in the form of anger. My youngest daughter is quoted in the very first line of the article when she said, "What's wrong with Daddy?"

Not exactly the way you want to be immortalized in the press, but this is such an important topic – depression and anger. Many people say, "My dad? Oh my gosh, I never saw my dad shed a tear. But come to think of it, he sure did yell a lot." Often, we think of depression as, "I'm just going to sit down and cry." Of course, sometimes that happens too. But we have a lot of officers that have severe anger issues, I believe often brought on by undiagnosed and untreated PTSD. In turn, we have a lot of officers that are depressed. By the way, this is not a male issue. Women have the same link between passive-aggressive anger and depression.

The feelings of rage are similar, but a little different. People who experience suicidal thoughts along with rage say things like, "I'll show them," or "I'll teach them not to treat me this way. When I'm gone, they'll be sorry." There is an irrational belief that killing yourself will make people that you feel wronged you feel bad. It's a powerful feeling, and one that I have experienced more times than I care to count.

Shame and Guilt. Guilt is the belief that you did something wrong, whether real or imagined. Guilt isn't always bad; it often keeps us from doing something we know we shouldn't do. Guilt and shame, however, are powerful emotions that can sometimes be predicated on false thinking. Has anyone ever apologized for things you have no control over? "I'm sorry it's raining." "I'm sorry the cable is out." Don't underestimate the way shame and guilt – real and false—can eat away at your heart and soul. Extreme feelings of guilt and shame led to thoughts of suicide that put me in the hospital, in 1996.

Worthlessness and hopelessness. We have all experienced feelings of worthlessness and hopelessness at some point in our lives. Nobody comes out of life unscathed. What is critical is how they play into suicide. In all the suicide interventions that I've done as well as my own thoughts of suicide, I have found in the vast majority of them—despite the situation or circumstance— the common denominators of feeling hopeless and worthless have been at the forefront of nearly every one of them. When these feelings are not addressed and combine with low self-esteem and self-confidence, suicide can readily come into the mix.

Expendability. Expendability is the feeling that you simply don't matter. In the movie, *Rambo: First Blood Part II* (TriStar Pictures, 1985), Rambo is sent on a mission where he is dropped into the Vietnamese jungle to find a POW camp and take pictures to show that no one is there. A local woman is his guide and as they're going down a jungle river in a boat, she asks, "Rambo, is that why they pick you? Because you like to fight?" He's sitting with his knife out, carving into the wood of the boat. "I'm expendable," he answers. She then asks him in her broken Vietnamese accent, "What mean expendable?" He explains, "You know, it's kind of like someone invites you to a party and you don't show up. It doesn't really matter."

When I started talking about the feelings of being expendable in my classes and using the Rambo story, it took me saying that line about 20 times until I didn't cry. I spent my life thinking that I was expendable and tried to use my career to prove otherwise. Many of us know what it's like to go to a party but still feel alone. Many of us wonder if it even matters that we're here today. Yes, it absolutely does matter. And it also matters that those feelings of being expendable can be a major indicator when it comes to feelings of suicide.

Extreme Sadness. Every one of us knows what it's like to feel sad. We know that clinical depression is more than just sadness, but sad feelings can become overwhelming. Extreme sadness can lead to the loss of joy. The loss of joy can lead to the loss of wanting to be alive.

Loneliness. Like shame and guilt, loneliness can be real or imagined. Like I just mentioned, we have all been to social gatherings and still felt alone even though we physically were not. Many people, however, feel alone because they actually are alone. I have known many officers that have gone through a divorce where they have lost everything. They go from living in a house with their wife and kids, to living alone in a studio apartment with every other weekend visitation with their children. Loneliness hurts. Loneliness is painful. And extreme feelings of loneliness can easily translate into feelings of suicide.

Loss/Grief. Loss and grief over what? Literally anything. Loss of a pet. Grief over the death of a parent. Loss of a loved one. Grief over failing grades. Loss of self-worth. Grief over losing a job. Demotion. Involuntary transfer. The list goes on and on. Can an officer be at risk of suicide if he or she lost a position on a specialized team, or was involuntarily transferred? I know I was. Can someone who is a straight A student in college be at risk for suicide because he or she received a B and now feels like a failure? Maybe. Is a mayor of a city at risk of suicide after being arrested for a DWI, knowing he's lost his status in the community? Possibly.

In the language of suicide, loss and grief are very significant indicators and triggers. It is important to remember that it is the perspective *of the person* who has experienced the loss that matters. Just because you might have lost a job and it didn't affect you to the point of thinking about suicide, doesn't mean that the loss of a job doesn't cause someone else to feel worthless and suicidal.

Ridicule by peers/bullying. Whether face-to-face or cyber-bullying, bullying and ridicule by peers can be a risk factor for suicide. As I mentioned in the chapter on police culture, bullying just doesn't happen in junior high school. It happens in every environment where there are people. People in schools, office buildings, police departments, nursing homes and everywhere in between experience bullying. Bullying does not necessarily cause suicide, but like I said, it can be a risk factor for suicide. Many people who are bullied don't take their own lives, and many people who have died by suicide were never bullied, but clearly it can be a risk factor.

Physical Appearance as the Language of Suicide

Not having any interest in their physical appearance. When you're thinking of killing yourself, who cares what you look like? I remember when I walked into my therapist's office in December 2014, just a few days before Christmas. I was horribly depressed and filled with anxiety and sadness. I usually went to my appointments looking fairly put together, but this time was different. The police-style military boots that I still wear were untied. I was wearing a raggedy sweatshirt that hadn't been washed and a very old baseball hat that had seen much better days. Because this was well outside my ordinary appearance, my therapist – in combination with other factors –knew that I was going to the hospital. An hour later, I was in the emergency room.

Change/loss in sex interest. A change in, or a loss of interest in sex can actually be an indicator of depression and possible suicidal thoughts. We will talk about this later in the book when I discuss relationships.

Sleep. Suicidal ideation and behaviors can be closely associated with sleep complaints, and in some cases, this association exists above and beyond depression. As a warning sign, recognizing disturbances in sleep, such as sleeping too much or too little, may be especially useful for suicide intervention efforts.

Eating habits/weight change. For some people stress and depression causes them to eat. For others, they experience loss of appetite. If you see someone in your life gaining or losing weight without trying, it can be an indicator of many things including suicidal thoughts.

Health Complaints as the Language of Suicide

More frequent headaches, colds, stomach problems, muscle aches, intensified physical and emotional fatigue, skin rashes, elevated blood pressure, cardiac problems, crying spells, or migraine headaches can be part of the unspoken language of suicide or people experiencing mental health issues. In one study, 69% of people who went to their primary care doctor for depression only reported their physical symptoms[25]. Physical symptoms are easier to talk about then crying yourself to sleep every night or constantly losing your temper. Stigma plays a huge role in this. That is one reason why the importance in training primary care physicians in the area of depression is so critical.

Actual Words as the Language of Suicide

It would be easy to identify someone who has thoughts of suicide if they just came up to you and said, "Hey, I feel like killing myself." But that's usually not how people initially talk about suicide. People say things like, "I can't take it anymore," "I wish I was dead," "I wish I was never born," "You'd all be better off without me," "I've got a way out of this," or "People are going to find out how bad things really are for me."

People can also get very theological when it comes to suicide. "Do you think heaven or hell is real?" "Do you think it hurts when you die?" "I'll be with my mom, who died three years ago. I'll be with her again soon."

Take any mention of death or suicide seriously, even if it's said flippantly. You've got to really hear and listen to these statements, and then ask some clarifying questions. Ask follow-up questions such as, "Can't take *what* anymore?" "Can you explain your *perfect* solution to me?" "Why won't you *need* that anymore?"

A Summary of Other Suicide Risks

When I train CIT officers on suicide intervention, I include a list of 'investigatory' questions that I have put together from various resources over the last 20 years that may help them determine whether or not a person is suicidal:

- Has the person been injured or attempted suicide? Injuries may include bruising around the neck, cuts on wrists, looking lethargic, etc.

- Has the person talked directly about suicide or wanting to die, to a family member? Direct statements of suicidal intent are strong indicators of the potential for suicide. In assessing for this factor, be aware of any statements of intent, even those made in a sarcastic or joking manner.

- Has the individual shown signs of depression? Depression is one of most common indicators for the potential of suicide. Common indicators of depression may include:
  - ✓ Extreme sadness, or crying.
  - ✓ Feeling more irritable, or angrier than usual.
  - ✓ Loss of interest in things that were once enjoyable.
  - ✓ Losing or gaining a significant amount of weight (not due to diet), or dramatic change in appetite.
  - ✓ Having trouble sleeping, or sleeping too much.
  - ✓ Physical feelings of either restlessness or being slow, sluggish.
  - ✓ Not having any energy.
  - ✓ Feeling of guilt (with no clear cause).
  - ✓ Not being able to concentrate or make decisions.
  - ✓ Thinking about wanting to end your life.

- Has the person experienced a stressful event? This is addressed in detail in the FAQ questions at the end of the chapter.

- Has the person begun making final arrangements, such as organizing wills and life insurance policies, reaching out to faith organizations regarding funerals, writing final letters to loved ones, etc?

- Does the person receive mental health treatment, or have they stopped seeing a mental health provider? As previously mentioned, 90% of those who die by suicide have a diagnosable mental health disorder at the time of their death. An individual in mental health treatment more than likely has an actual diagnosis of something. It would be important to ascertain who this is so they can be used as a follow up resource. Also, if the person has recently stopped seeing a mental health provider, it could lead to a decrease in their ability to cope with what is causing suicidal thoughts.

- Is the person taking mental health related medication? If so, has the person been taking it as prescribed? Stopping a mental health related medication can cause major psychological issues, which could include depression and thoughts of suicide.

Approaching Someone Who May Be Suicidal

When it comes to actually asking and talking about suicide, we need to recognize that the suicidal person is most commonly a person who is experiencing an acute psychiatric crisis, and is suffering from a mental health related issue. Thinking is often much distorted. It is important to remember that a person who has thoughts of suicide can be a danger to someone else—even if it's your dad, sister, or best friend. Your safety, and the safety of everyone involved, needs to be at the forefront of everyone's mind. The following information is a guide to how to approach someone who may be suicidal.

Asking the Question

Why don't people ask about suicide? That, in itself, is an important question. Countless times in their careers, law enforcement officers do inmate intakes and ask about suicide, or respond to a suicidal person call countless times. It's everyday stuff to ask about a suicide to a stranger during booking, or when responding to a call. But it is different when it's someone we know, work with, or love. There's personal emotion involved. Why do you think people have such a difficult time asking about suicide to their fellow officer or to their sister? I believe that the biggest reason is that they don't want to know the answer. We think, "What if they say 'yes'? Then what do I do?"

But asking the question is very important. How you do it, however, is equally important. Let's first discuss what you don't do. First, you don't ask the question in such a way that you get them to give you the answer that you want. You don't say while shaking your head no, "You're not going to do anything stupid, right?" "You're not going to do anything crazy, are you?" "You're not going to swallow your gun or anything, are you?" "You're not going to go off yourself, right?" That's how we tend to ask about suicide. We joke about it. "You're not going to do anything stupid, are you?" Obviously, what we want the person to say is, "No, I'm not," because we're uncomfortable with what the answer might be. Saying things like, "You're not thinking about doing anything stupid are you?" is unfortunately how many people ask about suicide. If asked in this manner, it's unlikely someone with thoughts of suicide will be honest with you. You have called them 'stupid' and told them what they should not be feeling. That is not likely to elicit an honest response.

Instead, when asking the question about suicide, you need to ask openly, honestly, and directly. You need to ask with compassion and empathy like you really want to know the answer. Ask, "Are you thinking about suicide?" "Are you thinking of killing yourself?" Many times, I've heard people say, "Isn't that kind of harsh and violent? Do I really need to use the word 'suicide' or 'kill'? What if I just ask, 'Are you thinking about hurting yourself?' What if I said that? Isn't that easier?"

My question back is, "Easier for whom?" If you are trying to make asking the question about suicide easy on you, then your focus is on the wrong person. Asking about suicide is not about you. It is about the person you are asking. Let's go back to the "Are you going to hurt yourself?" question. Is hurting and killing the same thing? Absolutely not. In a suicidal crisis, someone could ask me, "Eric, I need to ask you a question. Are you thinking about hurting yourself?" They could ask me with all the good intentions and with love in their heart, and I can look them right in the eye with every bit of honesty and integrity that I have. "Oh my gosh, hurt myself? I wouldn't dream of it. I'm not going to hurt myself. I guarantee you that." And then I would think, "I'm going to kill myself, but that's not what you asked me." It boils down to this—if you've got to ask the question about suicide, ask the damn question.

People often ask me, "Would people really be honest with you?" The answer is 'yes'—you'd be amazed at the amount of people who will answer, 'yes' when asked the question by someone who really cares about their response. There may be a part that wants to die, but there's still part that still wants to live. As I discussed, that's called suicide ambivalence and understanding it is invaluable. Without even saying a word to us, we know that the part that still wants to live is stronger than the part that wants to die, because they're still alive. They have yet to put their thoughts into action. They are still standing in front of you long enough for you to ask the question. That is a powerful thing to recognize and acknowledge.

When asking the question, be direct in a caring, non-confrontational way. Get the conversation started by describing the indicators that you have been made aware of, that would lead you to even be asking about suicide such as, "Your sergeant tells me that you've been pretty angry lately," or "I've heard about what's happening at work and how upset you are." The important thing is that you have got to start the conversation with something.

Ask openly, honestly, and directly about suicide while utilizing the indicators observed. Here is an example of phrasing I learned as an ASIST Master Instructor and have used countless times:

"Over the last few weeks, I've noticed that you've been pretty distant. I know you shared with me a little bit about what's going on at home, and I know that you didn't get

the promotion you were up for, again. You've also been talking about drinking more than usual, and the other day in the locker room you slammed your locker door and yelled, "I can't take this shit anymore." Sometimes when people start withdrawing from friends and family, have problems at home, start drinking more than usual, and say things like 'I can't take it anymore,' they sometimes think of suicide. Are you thinking about killing yourself?"

Let's break this statement down:

- You're telling someone who may be feeling worthless and expendable that you've been paying attention to him or her.

- You're telling that person that you care enough that you've noticed what he or she has been doing and are experiencing, and that you've heard what he or she has been saying. That's powerful to someone who feels like nobody cares.

- You're telling that person that not only have you noticed their behavior, but you're also telling them when some people show those behaviors, that they may be thinking of suicide. You've normalized suicide. You let them know that if they are thinking about suicide, then they are not alone in the world.

Do you need to have a Master's Degree in Psychology to ask if someone may be thinking about suicide; If you notice him or her withdrawing from friends and family; If you hear them saying they can't take it anymore; If they are having problems at home; If they are drinking more than usual? Of course not. You just have to care enough to notice, and then care enough to ask.

Yes or No Answers

If a person responds, "yes" that they are thinking of suicide, you would obviously stay connected with him or her and continue the conversation by asking follow-up questions. I'll get to those questions in a moment. First, it's important to discuss how people say 'yes' to the suicide question. If the person doesn't respond, shrugs his or her shoulders, or makes statements such as, "I don't know," or "Maybe," or "What difference would it make," then you must consider that the answer is 'yes'. Their inability to admit that they are having thoughts of suicide may be as clear as if they were openly admitting it.

Sometimes, people will answer, "no," but you may not be convinced that they are being truthful. Our intuition could tell us that they are not being honest. At that point, return to the list of indicators and ask the person the question about suicide again. "I hear that you're saying 'no', but this is what I'm seeing. I would hope that you would feel comfortable enough with me to tell me if that's how you're feeling." If the answer continues to be 'no; or if you believe that they are being truthful with their response, then offer continued and consistent support. Let them know you are there for them. Then actually be there for them. Provide resources to contact if they were to think of suicide. I have included a few resources at the end of this chapter.

If their answer is 'yes; in any form, stay connected and keep the person safe. This is not the time to debate about whether you think suicide is right or wrong, whether feelings are good or bad, what the value of life is, or whether you think their reasons for killing themselves is not really that big of a deal. Remember, it's not about you. Be willing to listen. A vast majority of people would be able to talk themselves out of suicide if they just had someone to listen to them; not give them advice, not try to fix it, not make it all better, not make them happy, not tell them a joke to ease the tension, but to just listen. That can be a very hard thing to do, but it's a vital part of your conversation.

Understanding A Person's Suicide Plan

If you have received a 'yes' response to the suicide question, it is imperative to ask about their plan, preparation, and time frame. Asking about a plan is a vital part of the asking process because not only will you know how at risk they are, but you'll also know what you'll need to do to disable their plan. Someone must disable the plan. I cannot emphasize that enough.

When we respond to a 911 call for a suicidal person with a gun, the first thing we do is take the gun. If it is overdose by pills, we take the pills. If a person is suicidal in a jail cell, we take their sheets. We do this as part of common procedure and common sense to simply prevent a suicide from happening. Unfortunately, we're much less quick to do this with a fellow member of law enforcement or a loved one. With all of my hospitalizations and suicidal behavior, I don't remember my department physically taking my gun away. Taking a cop's gun is often looked at as a sign of punishment or discipline, but when it comes to saving a life, take the gun(s), just like you would for anyone else.

Let me take you into my brain for a second so that you understand what happens when you have someone who has thoughts of suicide with the means of suicide so accessible to them. How many of you remember vinyl records and record players with their little needles? A record would scratch up and then skip and repeat itself. This is what happens with someone who has those continuous thoughts of suicide. This is what my mind did when I had my gun in my house. "Just go get it. Just go get it. It's right there. Just go get it. Just go get it. Just go shoot yourself. Shoot yourself. Shoot yourself. Just go get it. Just go get it. Just go get it." Over and over and over. After the gun is taken away, my brain literally stops the obsessive thought process, and I don't think about suicide anymore. If it's another means of suicide such as pills, my brain says, "Just go get them. Just go get them. Just take them." Over and over. If the pills are taken away, my brain stops thinking about suicide. Disabling someone's suicide plan by removing the actual method of suicide can actually help remove the thought of suicide. Many suicide prevention resources, including, as previously cited, the National Council for Behavioral Health's Mental

Health First Aid program, provide some questions to ask when talking with someone who is suicidal.

Ask openly and directly about a suicide plan; "Have you thought about how you would kill yourself?" Be sure to obtain as much detail as possible. There are countless ways to die by suicide. Whatever the response, acting shocked or saying things like, "That would be a horrible way to die!" will inevitably put distance between you and the individual. Please note that not having a specific plan does not mean that an individual is not serious about dying by suicide. Action must be taken with any individual that's threatening suicide, regardless of the presence of a specific plan. Having a plan puts someone at higher risk of suicide, but not having a plan doesn't mean there is no risk. A plan can take seconds to devise. We don't have the luxury of saying to ourselves, "No plan? She must not really mean it." That's a false belief.

It's also important to mention that the lethality of the plan does not matter a whole lot when it comes to taking thoughts or plans of suicide seriously. Imagine asking a young girl how she intends on killing herself and she responds, "I was going to take those five Tylenols I've been saving," We're pretty sure that would not actually cause someone to lose his life. However, I have actually had emergency room nurses say to people that I have brought into the ER for a suicide assessment, "Five Tylenols? That's not going to kill you. You'll need a lot more than that." Outrageous. Just because someone might be bad at pharmacology, does not mean his or her suicide attempt was any less valid.

The next crucial question is, "How ready are you to carry out this plan?" If a person's plan is with a firearm, my first question is, "Do you have a gun?" "Do you have bullets?" If the person's plan involves a knife, ask them "What knife?" If it involves asphyxiation, ask them "What are you planning to use to hang yourself?" If it involves driving a car off a cliff, ask them "What car are you planning on using and what cliff are you thinking about?" It's crucially important to get as much specific detail about the plan as possible, because it's the only way you will be able to properly disable it.

Next, get a timeline. "How soon are you planning on killing yourself?" If the answer is, "Right after you leave," we know the risk is extremely imminent and our actions of keeping the person safe will need to be imminent as well. If the person says next week or after my last child goes off to college, our actions may not have to be so imminent, but they cannot in anyway be delayed or put off either. Plans can change in the blink of an eye.

One issue that gets rarely addressed in suicide prevention programs is that after you have asked about the individual's plan of suicide, it is imperative that you ask the individual if there is a second, third, fourth, or more plans. Many people who have thoughts of suicide and have developed a plan to actually use it, also may have one or more back-up plans, should the first one not work or is no longer an option. I currently have eight solid plans on how to die by suicide. In a crisis, if someone asks me about one, I will give them one. But if I am not asked about second, third, fourth, etc., chances are I'm not going to offer it up. The most suicide plans I have ever discovered were from a 12-year-old who was suicidal. He had nine plans. He couldn't explain them verbally to me, but he showed me the pictures of his plans that he had drawn in a notebook. If there is more than one plan, each needs to be asked with the questions to determining different accessibility and time frames. If suicide plan(s) are provided, take all action(s) necessary to disable each plan whenever possible, as long as it is safe for you to do so. I know that asking if there are additional plans has helped save lives. It is similar to when I used to teach defensive tactics and trained officers to pat someone down. If we find one weapon, we always assume there is another one. The same thing with suicide plans, always assume there is another one until proven otherwise.

After Asking the Question

Do not leave the person alone. For the most part, suicide is a very private thing. Even though there have been situations in which people have died by suicide in public, it is still very rare. Leaving the person alone even for an instant can obviously give the person the opportunity to kill himself/herself, or to run out the back door. This can lead to all types of challenging issues.

Never reject the person's feelings of worthlessness, hopelessness, or helplessness. Do not say things like, "Oh, it's not that bad," "Look at all you have to live for." "What do you mean you feel alone? You have like 1,000 friends on Facebook." Empathetic statements such as, "I'm sorry you feel so alone," go a lot further than telling someone their feelings don't matter.

Do not pressure the person to move at a specific pace. Signs of depression and suicidal intentions can be a marked loss of energy, being unable to concentrate, or make decisions. Pressure put on an individual to rush or move quickly will likely increase the person's level of stress, and result in a less than positive experience for all involved.

Never dare him or her to do it. What? Someone would actually do that? Yes. I've heard things like, "A real man would have done it by now." I remember a class I taught at a church many years ago, and this point of not daring people to kill themselves came up. After the class, a woman told me a story about her son. He had been mentally ill, and in and out of the hospital for years. He had talked about killing himself often, and she mentioned that she and her family would constantly work hard to help keep him from acting on it. Then she started to tear up as she began to tell me about what had happened one fateful day. Her son had once again talked about killing himself over and over, and wouldn't stop. This woman—this frustrated mom—said to him, "Just do it already. I can't take you talking about this anymore!" She looked at me with tears streaming down her face and told me that those were the last words she ever said to her son. Did she want him to kill himself? Of course not. Out of frustration, anger, or whatever she was feeling, she inadvertently gave him the permission he may have been looking for. My heart absolutely broke for this mom. I'll never forget that.

Don't try to fix it or make everything all better. In doing so, you're dismissing the feelings the person is having, and ignoring the actual suicidal crisis the person is experiencing. Chances are that what he or she is experiencing can't be "fixed" by just saying the right thing. Your role at this point is to simply be there for the person.

Never tell him or her that everything will be okay. Why? Simply because you don't know if everything will be ok. Whatever situation they are experiencing may actually get worse as the days pass. Instead of saying this very glib statement that people say because it sounds nice, saying something like, "No matter what happens, I'm here for you," is much more comforting. The thing is, however, that if you are going to tell someone you're going to be there for them, make sure that you are.

Top Questions I Have Been Asked About Suicide

After more than 20 years working in suicide prevention, especially in law enforcement, there are questions that I have been repeatedly asked. I'd like to share the questions and my answers with you.

What if I'm not the person to ask the question? In law enforcement, whether working on the streets or in a corrections setting, we ask people about suicide all the time. But it's different when it's someone you know. When it's someone we care about, we feel awkward, nervous, and reluctant to ask the question about suicide. So, we do other things like talk about happy things, or invite someone out for a drink to relax when in reality, someone needs to ask that person about suicide. If you're not the person to ask that question, please know that is okay. If you can't ask the question with confidence, with what to do if they say, "yes," that's fine. But what you must do, without delay, is find someone who can ask. When someone is giving indications of suicide, not asking is not an option. Tell someone else, whom the person is close to, what you are observing and what indications you have seen that suicide might be an issue. Be brave enough to admit that it's hard for you to ask the question. If you can't ask, that's ok. Just please find someone who can.

Does everyone thinking of suicide have to go to the hospital? That's a huge question for law enforcement officers. On our job, we know that if someone mentions suicide, we are legally bound to take them to the hospital or get put on 24-hour watch. We are not so quick, however, to want to take or force a fellow officer or a family member to go to a psychiatric emergency room. Psychiatric emergency rooms and possible subsequent hospitalizations are there for one purpose—to keep the person from killing themselves. Most hospitalizations are short-term until the suicide crisis passes, and the person feels safe to return home. It shouldn't be this way, but the reality is that a psychiatric hospitalization could potentially have a very negative impact on an officer's career. Not everyone needs to be taken to a hospital. If a person can be kept safe by not being left alone, and by removing any means of suicide, referred to professionals and given as much personal support as possible, they *may* not have to go to a hospital. The time when hospitalization is a must is when that individual cannot be kept safe, is adamant about dying, and needs a secure facility. Whatever the case, I cannot reiterate enough the importance of connecting that person with a professional as soon as possible. There can be no mistake that that must happen.

Should I protect his or her confidentiality? This seems obvious, right? Of course, thoughts of suicide can't be kept confidential. You can't ask someone about suicide and then promise that you won't tell anyone if they say 'yes'. In fact, in all my suicide interventions over the years, one of the most important questions I ask the person is, "Who else besides me should know about this?" Not letting loved ones or trusted friends know is not an option. You absolutely should not be the only person to know this potentially life-threatening information. It's not fair to the person in crisis, and it's not fair for you to have the weight of that responsibility on yourself alone. You want that person to have as much support around them as possible. With my six hospitalizations while on the job, I was terrified that everyone would know. "Please don't tell anyone," was a common statement. In my hospitalizations, however, only the people that needed to know knew. As I've shared, my supervisors and my close friends kept my business as my business. As officers, and as people, spreading rumors and false information is something we do well. This is not the time. Enough said.

What about their gun? I've addressed this earlier, and I believe it is so important that I'll address it again. The one thing I don't remember my department doing was taking my gun. I've asked my old supervisors and even my wife at the time, but it was so long ago, I get conflicting accounts. What I do know is that my then wife took my gun several times. I remember fighting over it one time in my garage. This short question requires a short answer. Take their damn gun, or in most cop's cases, guns. I'm not saying that they have to be confiscated and turned into the property clerk's office like evidence, but someone needs to get them away from the person at risk. Whether it's a fellow officer or an uncle, someone must remove the firearms and/ or whatever other means the person at risk has identified as a means of suicide. It's unbelievable that when we respond to calls where someone is threatening suicide and is in possession of a shotgun, we take it without a second thought. But when it comes to removing an officer's gun, we hesitate and think that it'll be viewed as some kind of punishment. As I've mentioned and I'll mention again, you're not removing it as a punishment, but to literally help save their life.

What if they refuse my help? When it comes to people who are having thoughts of suicide and they tell you to leave them alone, we don't have the luxury of saying, "Well, I tried." You must tell someone else immediately and without hesitation. A person's life is at risk. Telling someone else when a person refuses help is not the same as spreading rumors, it's literally about potentially saving a life. If someone is at immediate risk of suicide, you may in fact need to call 911. I've had the police called on me twice, and it was the right thing to have been done at the time.

In Conclusion

This has been a long chapter—the longest in the entire book. It is so because suicide is the number one killer of law enforcement, and at epidemic numbers throughout America. I hope you get the message that suicide is preventable, and suicidal thoughts are common. I hope you get the message that asking the question about suicide openly, honestly, and directly is vital and getting help for that person that says 'yes' is critical.

I mention this in all my classes, and sometimes it's a hard thing to say but important for people, especially suicide loss survivors, to hear. Sometimes, we can do all the right things, say all the right things, and ask all the right questions, and sometimes people still die by suicide. That is a sad fact and a sad reality for some, and has been a reality for me. However, I do know that mental illnesses are treatable, recovery is possible, and most importantly, *suicide is preventable.* If I didn't believe that with all my heart, then this entire chapter and the last 20 years of life is in vain. Finally, if you are experiencing thoughts of suicide, get help. If someone you know or love is experiencing these thoughts, offer it.

One of the major reasons why we don't respond to suicidal thoughts and attempts is because of the stigma associated with mental illness, as was discussed earlier.

Crisis Resources

NATIONAL SUICIDE PREVENTION HOTLINE
1-800-273-8255 (TALK)
(*Veteran's Press 1)

Crisis Text Line
Text "HOME" to 741741

SAFE CALL NOW: 206-459-3020. A 24-hour *confidential* crisis referral service for all police public safety employees, all emergency services personnel and their family members nationwide.

COPLINE: | AN OFFICER'S LIFELINE International Law Enforcement Officers' Hotline: A 24-hour *confidential* crisis referral service for all police public safety employees personnel and their family members nationwide.
1-800-COPLINE
1-800-267-5463

The Badge of Life
www.badgeoflife.com

National P.O.L.I.C.E. Suicide Foundation
www.psf.org

Resources-References

American Foundation for Suicide Prevention
www.afsp.org
Toll-Free: 1-888-333-AFSP (2377)

American Association of Suicidology
www.suicidology.com
5221 Wisconsin Avenue, NW, 2nd Floor
Washington, DC 20015
T: (202) 237-2280,

National Institute of Mental Health
Office of Science Policy, Planning, and Communications
6001 Executive Boulevard, Room 6200, MSC 9663
Bethesda, MD 20892-9663
1-866-615-6464
www.nimh.nih.gov/health/statistics/suicide

Recommended Additional Mental Health/Suicide Intervention Training:

Mental Health First Aid for Public Safety
National Council for Behavioral Health
www.mentalhealthfirstaid.org

Applied Suicide Intervention Skills Training
LivingWorks
www.livingworks.net

CHAPTER 13

SHINING THE LIGHT ON FAMILY

I may be the last person you would want to listen to about family relationships. After all, by the time I was 25, I had been married twice and had two children. The first marriage at age 20 lasted about a year, and the second at age 23 lasted 24 years—much to my surprise. For the first three and a half decades of my life, my career, mental health, bad choices, and overall immaturity had a lot to do with the end of these marriages. At age 48, I got married for a third time to my current wife, Lynne, and it has been a wonderful eight years (and I'm not just saying that because she's looking over my shoulder as I write). I have three grown children, one from my first marriage and two from my second. When Lynne added her two teenagers to the mix, I got a crash course in step-parenting. For the most part, today I have good, and sometimes not so good relationships with my three kids and two step-kids, as well as with my seven grandkids. It has not always been that way and it's a continual journey for sure.

Actually, when I think about it, because of all my good and bad experiences with life and family, I probably can shine some light on this topic quite well. Believe me, talking about family relationships is very important in exploring suicide, trauma and mental illness among law enforcement. Marriages and relationships are hard in general, let alone when one or both individuals are in law enforcement. In our profession, divorce, extra-marital affairs, child custody disputes, and family financial issues are common. Although I can't specifically quote the source, I've heard it said that nearly 80% of law enforcement marriages end in divorce. Based on the officers that I have worked with, that number seems pretty accurate.

The most startling statistic for me is this one: At least 40% of police officer families experience domestic violence in the form of physical, emotional, verbal, sexual, and financial abuse in contrast to 10% of families in the general population.[1] I vividly remember handling my very first domestic violence complaint against a fellow officer. As a brand-new sergeant, I answered a 2 a.m. complaint call, which I assumed would be someone getting a parking ticket they didn't think they deserved or complaining that one of my officers was rude to them. Unfortunately, it wasn't that simple. When I pulled up to the apartment complex, a young and very upset woman with facial injuries came running towards my car. "My boyfriend beat me up, and I know you're not going to do anything about it because he's a cop," she said. My first thought? "Oh, shit." When she told me who he was, I had never heard the name before. I learned that he was a recruit in the middle of field training and then went to talk to him, but he ran out the back door of his townhouse without me seeing him, otherwise I probably would have gotten into a foot chase with a police recruit. After taking the victim to the hospital for treatment, I called my staff duty officer, filed a crime report listing the recruit as the suspect, took a deposition and personnel complaint from the victim, and wrote a very lengthy and detailed internal report on what had transpired. Needless to say, this recruit, whom I literally never met or laid my eyes on, didn't have a job the next day. Unfortunately, this wouldn't be the only time in my career that I dealt with fellow officers who were domestic violence offenders.

What about myself? I've been open with you throughout this book, and I will continue to do so. I can honestly say that throughout my marriages, I never once hit my wives or kids. I may have patted a behind here and there, but I never remember ever spanking my children. Please know that I am not looking for extra credit or praise for not hitting my wives and kids. You don't get extra credit for not doing what you shouldn't be doing in the first place. What I did, however, wasn't much better. Instead of hitting members of my family, I ruled my home through fear and intimidation. If I didn't want to talk, I would yell and throw a chair. If I wanted the conversation to end, I'd yell and try to punch a hole in the wall. My family was kind of afraid of me. I wasn't a very nice dad all the time. Needless to say, my family suffered, and I deeply apologize to each of them for my behavior.

Challenges Faced by Law Enforcement at Home

So why does this breakdown of the family happen? What can we do about it? Let me start by addressing some of the issues and challenges I have experienced and observed.

We learn to not show emotion. Showing emotion, even with your own family, is a perceived sign of weakness. When I first became a husband and father, I was already in the law enforcement culture. It took only a couple of months on the job, but I quickly learned that showing emotion was sternly frowned upon by my co-workers. That behavior seeped into my home life. For example, I played the role of a strong father, never letting my daughters see me cry. I only wanted them to see my tough outer shell of strength. I was neither sympathetic nor empathetic as a husband or father. Instead, I was impatient, overbearing, and yelled all the time. My attempt at never showing anything but a rock-solid exterior to my family failed miserably. All of that pent-up emotion had to come out at some point. Since my first hospitalization back in 1996, my daughters have seen me cry more times than I can count. On more than one occasion over the years, I have actually called them crying hysterically during a crisis, and they helped bring me down from that spiral. I am so eternally grateful for them, but I put them in a position where they should not have to be.

We often only show emotions like anger, rage, jealousy or hostility. I think there's a simple explanation as to why this is true—those emotions are really easy. Why in the world would I want to sit down and talk about stuff when I can just get angry and simply make my wife not want to talk to me? It takes no thought whatsoever to get angry—discipline and scream at your kids, be jealous because some girl looked at your husband or boyfriend, or just be generally hostile to everyone around you. It takes time and effort to sit down and have a meaningful conversation. I figured I could just be an asshole and...problem solved! In reality, I solved nothing, but made my first two wives miserable, not to mention my children. Yes, the emotions listed above are easy, but as I've matured, I've learned that love can come pretty easy too. It's just a matter of what type of husband/father/wife/mother you really want to be.

We must always be in control. A few of the synonyms for the word control are "command, keep under control, and influence." That's pretty much exactly what we do in law enforcement. Whether you're putting someone in a cell or the back of your car, you need to be in control. Matter of fact, you'd better be in control otherwise you're in the wrong profession. Unfortunately, many officers, including myself, took and still take the word, "control" too literally on calls or during arrests. There are real limits to the control we can demonstrate on the job and whether we like it or not, the world is watching. In my view, that is a good thing, even though it does make our jobs much harder at times.

What about at home? I personally felt that since I was in control at work and in charge of many officers—especially after being promoted to sergeant in 1992—then I would be damned if I wasn't going to be in charge at home as well. Here was my thinking: "You know something, honey? I'm at charge in work, and I'm in charge at home. If you or the kids question whether or not I'm in charge, you're all going to find out pretty quickly that I am." I don't know if I ever uttered those exact words out loud, but I certainly know I felt them, and all too often demonstrated them. As I mentioned, statistics surrounding domestic violence in law enforcement percentages are so high, and I'm pretty sure that this issue of control is a huge part of the reason.

A healthy relationship is not a dictatorship; it is a partnership where both individuals are equal, neither better nor more in charge than the other. Both work together to make a strong bond. It's funny (but not so funny) that even writing those words make me shake my head. Back in the day, if you were to tell me that I would someday think that marriage was a partnership, I would have literally laughed in your face. Unfortunately, there are too many of us that still struggle tremendously in this area.

We act like we don't care. It's not unusual for a spouse to ask, "Hey honey, I know you have tomorrow night off. Would you like to go out to dinner? Any place special?" Often, we respond, "I don't care" because we don't have a preference. That's pretty common behavior. There is another kind of "I don't care" answer, however, that is destructive to relationships and families. Again, it's that apathetic response when you stop caring about what is happening in your life, or in the lives of the people around you. In my depressive and suicidal state, I didn't care if I lived or died. Do you really think I cared if we went to Applebee's or Chili's that night for dinner? Do you really think I cared that we were out of milk or a bill was late?

But you don't have to be depressed or suicidal to dismiss you family and come across as indifferent. After so many life and death matters at work, dealing with the little things in life start to not matter. You lose interest in what's happening around you and with the people you love the most. You give the impression that you don't care about what you do together as a family or who drives the kids to the soccer game or birthday party. Often, it's too late for a healthy family life to recover when we finally realize that those little things were actually the things that mattered most.

We stop communicating. This was a typical week of conversations with my wife when I was a police officer:

<u>Monday</u>

"Hi honey, how was your night?"

"Fine."

"Anything happen?"

"Nope."

"Anything you want to talk about?"

"Nope."

<u>Tuesday</u>

"Hi honey, how was your night?"

"Fine."

"Anything happen?"

"Nope."

"Anything you want to talk about?"

"Nope."

<u>Wednesday – Friday</u>

See above.

Do you see the pattern? Year after year, I responded to my wife in the same way. Then after a while she would ask, "Why don't you and I ever talk anymore? You don't talk to me, and you barely talk to the kids. What's wrong?" My answer was always the same. "I just don't feel like it." Let me assure you, I am not unique among officers. Many – men and women – respond the same way. One might only imagine the conversations between spouses that are both in law enforcement.

The result of this lack of communication is that we become alienated from our families and loved ones. It starts to feel like we live alone even if the house is full. Because I didn't talk much to my family, I started to feel isolated and separated from them. I was just some guy who just happened to live in a house with other people in it. And surprise, surprise—the less I would talk to my wife and kids, the less they would talk to me. Then I'd get angry because I didn't know what was happening in my own house. The cycle would repeat itself over and over again.

Just imagine, for example, if my conversation had gone like this with my wife.

"Hi honey, how was your night?"

"It was alright, pretty busy though."

"Anything happen?"

"Lots. Seems like people are just so angry all time. What I wouldn't give to go to a call where I feel like people actually want me there."

"Anything you want to talk about?"

"Kind of. This last week has been really hard. Do you mind if I talk to you about all that's happening?"

I'm not naïve enough to think that many of you feel you can talk that way. In fact, I suspect that you may have read the revised conversation, rolled your eyes, and thought how stupid it sounded. But we need to start doing something else besides "how was your night/fine" communication with those we love and who love us back. If you are still skeptical about having real conversations, my questions to you are simple. "How's that working for you? Does it make you feel closer to your spouse or significant other? Do you feel like you just live in a house with other people you really don't know?" I'm fairly certain that we all know the answers.

The value of communication among families, partners, friends and anyone you care about cannot be overemphasized.

Being able to be open and honest in your relationships is a key skill to how we live our lives. The right way to communicate, however, doesn't come automatically; often it is a learned skill that depends on the situation. Many of us are great communicators at work, but don't know how to talk to our own kids or other people. I know this because I teach communication skills during Crisis Intervention Training, which deals with interacting with those in a mental health crisis. I have spent years building up my own communication skills as part of my job and my family life, but as my kids can attest to, sometimes I still fail miserably. It is a skill I need to constantly relearn and refine.

We take family for granted. I truly felt that no matter how I acted, what I did, and how I spoke or behaved, my family would always be there. I was the main breadwinner and provided financial security. I figured that I was so awesome that they would never leave. I was seriously wrong. I had an affair once and my wife at the time left, but she always forgave me. Midway through my marriage to her, I realized that my behavior was destroying my relationship with her and our children. I started to change, and finally in 2000, when faith became part of my life, I understood how a spouse and family should be treated. But it was too late. Too much damage had been done. The years taking her and the family for granted, and her reactions to it, finally caught up with us, and we ended up splitting up. I know that many of us have told ourselves the lie that our family will always be there no matter what we do. I thought that for decades. Now with nearly eight years of marriage to my third wife, Lynne, and a lot more life under my belt, I've learned to never take anything for granted. What's here today may be gone tomorrow.

We lose sexual intimacy. When sexual intimacy—not necessarily simply the act of sex—begins to suffer, it can often be an indicator of a problem within a relationship. As a pastor, I worked in a church with a 1,100-person congregation and did the majority of pastoral care and counseling. Couple after couple came in and discussed their challenges and difficulties, and

I found that quite often one common denominator was about intimacy. Because it came up so often, I actually took a Christian class on human sexuality and I started being proactive in asking some hard questions. When speaking with couples during a counseling session, I would wait a half hour while they complained and screamed at each other. Then I would say, "Do you mind if I ask you a really difficult and personal question? This might sound really weird coming from your pastor, but can you tell me the last time the two of you were intimate with each other?"

Without fail, the answer was a loud, "I don't know" or "What, it's been like six months, a year? Who even keeps track anymore?" or "Tell him to stop treating me like crap and to stop yelling at the kids all the time, then maybe I'll eventually want to sleep with him again." Then the other half would reply, "You know something, if she would just stop nagging me all the time about everything and stop telling me everything I do is wrong, then maybe I would actually want to be with her again." When I address this point in my classes, I carefully watch the reaction of the officers who are in attendance. You would be amazed at the number of officers who look down, put their hands to their face, or simply shake their head. I know that I hit a nerve. Sexual intimacy is a crucial part of any healthy relationship. If you and your partner are finding this to be an issue, it's time to have an open and honest discussion or seek professional help.

We use humor and cynicism. I've discussed our coping skill of cop humor and how it isn't healthy. When we bring cop humor home, our loved ones don't usually appreciate it as much as we might think they do. They don't understand how we see or talk about the world around us; why we think the misery of others is funny; and why it seems like we dislike everyone. They think that the way we laugh about things isn't really funny. Our cynicism seems unwarranted and mean. How many times have you heard, "You know, that's really not funny. You actually really sound like a jerk when you talk that way. Who are you anymore?"

When Home Is Not Home Anymore

How do all these factors play into the balance between home and work life? Let me tell you that they have a tremendous effect. I know a lot of officers who literally work 10, 20, 30, and even 40 hours of voluntary overtime a week. The key word is voluntary, as I know mandatory overtime is a reality for many. When I ask why they volunteer for so much overtime, they often give a pat answer like, "Well, you know I just bought that new boat," "I just got that new truck," "I've still got kids in school and have to pay for college," or "I just love my job." Then I ask them to be honest and tell me why they are really working so much overtime. The answers often change: "Because I don't want to go home. You know what it's like to be at my house? We fight all the time, and the kids are always asking for something. Who wants to go home? It's just easier to hang out with my buddies. It's easier to just work, compared to going home."

If any of those statements ring true for you as they did for me, it's time to be honest with yourself. If you're having those conversations or thoughts, it's time to do some self-reflecting or have an open conversation with someone. Unfortunately, you may find out that because of your neglect, your family doesn't want you there anyway, and you have serious work to do. My adult daughters have had some painful but healthy discussions with me over these last many years, about what it was like growing up. "Dad, you know when you would call Mom and tell her you had to work overtime, and that we wouldn't see you until the next day or two? Sometimes, we were actually relieved that you weren't coming home." Let me tell you, it is a very humbling experience to have your children tell you that they were glad when you weren't home. It is a hard thing to hear, but it can serve as a huge wake up call.

I often give my class attendees an optional homework assignment, where they gather their family around the table or living room and ask them a question. Officers are requested to clearly state to their family that no matter what answer they get, they will not get mad. The question the officers are tasked with asking is simply this: "Are you happy when I'm home?" Many officers who hear this assignment think, "That's a stupid ass question. Are you happy when I'm home? That's ridiculous. Who's going to ask that question?" My question back to them is, "Do you know why you think it's a stupid question?" because I believe they either know the answer or are afraid of what it will be. Many of us don't want an honest answer to this very powerful question because we just don't want to hear it. The truth is that sometimes hard questions can open a dialogue that otherwise may never occur. Honest answers can create an environment that generates real conversations that allow relationships to heal with the people you love the most. Over the years, I have observed that when officers went home and asked the question to their families, their responses fell into two categories: One group found out that they weren't as bad as they thought they were, and their family actually enjoyed it when they were home. The other group had this kind of response: "You know, I went home and asked that question. My wife and I were up until 2 a.m. talking about things we have never talked about before."

I'd like everyone who is reading this book to ask your family that question, "Are you happy when I am home?" While I designed the exercise for law enforcement officers, it is beneficial for all families. I personally still check in and ask that question of my wife and family. Today, it's really nice to hear how much they usually love it when I'm around. It's taken a lot of work on my part, and theirs as well, but it is so worth it.

The "I Don't Bring My Work Home with Me" Myth

Another question I ask my class is, "How many of you have ever had a bad day at work and took it out on someone at home?" Whether I'm teaching officers, nurses, or even faith leaders, nearly every hand goes up. While many of us do not actually "talk" about work at home, that doesn't mean we're not bringing it home. Whether it is yelling about a toy left on the stairs or withdrawing and just being silent, we're bringing our work home with us. You may have heard it said, "Wherever you go, there you are." I can't stress enough that even if we don't talk about work, we're inevitably bringing it home somehow. So how can you bring your work home and not have it destroy your relationships? Consider having an open conversation with trained professionals or people around you, where you actually talk about how you are feeling. Don't have a bitch session with fellow officers. That does not work and can actually exasperate your frustration, which will come out at home. Instead, get honest and real.

What about having an argument at home and then taking it out on someone at work? Most people in my classes raise their hand in agreement on this one too. We bring home life into our work—from yelling at someone when making an arrest, to giving someone an extra ticket that we didn't really need to. I remember one officer whose use of force increased every time he had a fight with his wife. When he and his wife were getting along, his use of force was almost non-existent. Unfortunately, he and his wife fought too much.

What about Female Officers and Their Families?

Remember Sergeant Kiersten Harzewski from my chapter on stressors and the police culture? Here is her incredible valuable perspective on women in law enforcement and family:

When my husband started his career in law enforcement, his parents were proud. My family was proud. Our daughter was 18 months old, and I was pregnant with our second daughter while he was at the police academy. I was expected to hold it together while he moved his career forward. Job, pregnancy, toddler, and home responsibilities were expected of me during this time. However, when the roles were reversed, holding it together with the girls and me going to the academy, I was a neglectful mother not considering the impact of this dangerous profession on my children. Five years later, after infidelity and financial problems, we got divorced. Those problems did not exist prior to me joining the job.

Female officers have an added challenge when it comes to maintaining their "role" in law enforcement and at home. Traditionally speaking, when a man chooses police work, goes to the academy, is away from his family for weeks at a time, long shifts, tough assignments, etc., he is providing for his family. This is an honorable profession, and his family is proud. Traditionally, when a woman does the same thing, regardless of the challenges of the profession, she is putting her family on the back burner. She is putting a dangerous career in front of her family, jeopardizing her life, and leaving her children and husband unattended. When a male officer does it, he is a provider. When a female officer does it, she is labeled as a career woman, a selfish woman, or maybe even an absent mom.

Adding that perspective, or that battle if you will, on top of the day to day trauma that we face as officers, can make a woman doubt her judgment. If her child is acting out and she isn't home because she is handling a call of someone else's child acting out, it can make her doubt her commitment to her family and have to deal with the judgment that comes from her family because of it. A male officer misses Thanksgiving because he has to work. That's part of the job. A woman misses Thanksgiving because she has to work, and she is judged harshly by those at home. Who is going to make the turkey, coordinate the meal, and facilitate a warm and loving family environment?

Now, I've been married three times, with two daughters from my first marriage, and one daughter from my *second marriage. Sadly, most husbands aren't prepared for the lifestyle that comes with being a female officer. I often wondered what kind of mother risks leaving her children possibly orphaned for a job. What happens if I am killed at work? Yes, death is a possibility for all of us. But this job does increase the odds. Leaving my children, risking my life, missing school functions, bringing germs and disease home on my uniform, I could go on and on. But from a woman's perspective – it adds to the weight of managing the trauma we face on the job. I'm now in my third marriage of almost 15 years to another officer, be-cause it really is the only relationship that works."*

What About the Children?

This chapter has focused primarily on adult relationships. The real family victims of cumulative stress, trauma and mental illness, however, are often the children. The mood swings and anger create a very unstable environment where the kids are often scared and worried about what will tick Mom or Dad off. The isolation and withdrawal are often even more devastating for children, because they begin to believe that something is wrong with them – that they are unlovable and that's why their parent is absent from their lives. It has taken more than 20 years to rebuild relationships with my children whom I fiercely love, and I'm still trying desperately to repair the damage I've caused. Nothing is more important to me than their happiness and protection. Unfortunately, for many years, I simply was not able to do that. As I have mentioned, they have talked with me often about what it was like growing up with me. It was not easy to hear.

Additionally, there are genetic elements to mental illness. Scientists have long recognized that many psychiatric disorders tend to run in families. One of the most difficult times relating to my own mental illness history occurred when I learned that a couple of my daughters were dealing with their own mental health issues, from mild and moderate to severe. I know some of it is genetic, some is situational, and some of it is also because of the way they grew up.

Here I was, a big tough sergeant, and I hadn't been able to protect my own children from their own mental health struggles. I have forgiven myself for the most part, but I have not forgotten. Neither have they.

Living with someone who is mentally ill

Lynne and I have a wonderful marriage. But she reminds me that she didn't marry an on-duty cop, but a retired one since we got married seven years after my retirement. I'm not the same person now as I was back then. And, for that, we are all grateful.

But living with me and my mental illness isn't easy. One example is that my PTSD has on-going effects. When I sleep, I have horrible nightmares that cause me to physically lash out. My PTSD nightmares consist of being on the job and fighting a criminal. I told you earlier that during these unconscious hours, I have hit, pushed, pulled her hair, and punched her. When she wakes me up, I feel horrible and apologize profusely. Her reaction is the same: "You didn't want this to happen either, and it's not your fault." She shows me lots of grace and mercy.

However, not everyone does. I have had some difficult times in the past with the friends and family I'm closest to, enough so that it has led me to suicidal thoughts. It's clearly not anyone's fault that I feel suicidal, but whenever those thoughts have been triggered, I have thought about suicide and have come all too close to acting upon it. Please be careful with those within your friends, family or circle of influence who are struggling with their mental health. They may be more vulnerable than you think.

When I have an episode, whether I'm crying, feeling suicidal, or frustrated with my mental health, Lynne reminds me,

"You didn't do anything wrong. Mental illness is a medical condition. You don't deserve this, and we'll work through this together."

And we do. We work to keep me healthy, us healthy. I see a therapist, a psychiatrist, take my medications, exercise, and recently added ketamine infusions. It is important to keep trying to move forward, because recovery is ongoing therapy. I can't afford to stop.

Unfortunately, people do stop taking care of themselves because they perceive that they are fine, even though their actions indicate that they are off balance. And a downward spiral can ensue, causing harm in both adult and child relationships.

One Last Thought

In my career, I bled, sweated, and dedicated my life to my job, working extra-long hours, midnights, and making literally thousands of arrests. My job came before everything else. Now I've been retired for 15 years, and with retirements and turnover rates, there are hundreds of officers in my department who have never heard my name and can literally say, "Eric Weaver who?" I've mentioned this before, and I'll repeat it as much as I need to. The job that I dedicated my life to is over. But what remains after all that time? My family; the ones whom I ignored all of those years.

Someday, there will be a point in time when you will no longer be in law enforcement. There will be a point in time when the people in your department won't even know who you are. I challenge you to check your priorities before any more time passes and there are more regrets. I love my life now, but like many of us, I wish I could go and turn back the clock. I know the way I did life would be much different. What I do know is that it is never too late.

For those of you who are married, divorced, or single, I hope that this chapter has helped you gain a better understanding of the complexities of the law enforcement family. It's challenging to say the least, but the more we know about the realities of it, the more we can make a positive difference in the people that matter most.

CHAPTER 14

ACHIEVING AND MAINTAINING EMOTIONAL HEALTH

Achieving and maintaining emotional health requires work. Many of us look in the mirror after taking a shower and admit that we've gained a few pounds and need to start losing weight. We look at ourselves and know that we need to shave or get a haircut. These, of course, are all superficial and, at the end of the day, really don't matter. What matters is how we see ourselves on the inside, but, unfortunately, many of us don't really want to see what's going on. Without that introspection, it is very difficult to stay emotionally healthy. Just like my rust spot analogy back in the Cumulative Stress chapter, we spray paint over it again and again, hoping no one sees, especially ourselves. Although it takes work, you can take action to achieve and maintain emotional health. Here are eight core principles that I have developed over many years from talking with thousands of people about emotional health. I believe they can help you frame how to best help yourself and those around you.

Principle #1: Know That You Have Worth and Value.

As a child or adult, feelings of worthlessness and hopelessness can plague us. Most people have experienced these feelings at some point in their life. Every time I was hospitalized, for example, my own feelings of value and worth were non-existent. Additionally, so many things I did in my life, like being on SWAT and 22 years in law enforcement, were accomplishments to help me alleviate my feelings of worthlessness. I wanted people to see value in me, even if I didn't see it in myself.

One of the most common denominators in every suicidal person that I have ever dealt with – no matter their circumstance and situation—was an extreme sense of worthlessness. So, while the vast majority of people struggle with self-esteem and self-confidence when they look in the mirror, knowing that each one of us has value and worth changes how we look at one another, and equally important, ourselves. Your feelings of value and worth cannot be underestimated. That's why it's the #1 Principle. Despite how we feel at any given time, it's important to know that our feelings often lie. Just because we "feel" a certain way, doesn't necessarily make it true. Every one of us needs to know that we have value. We need to understand that our life means something outside of our profession, despite how we see ourselves.

And what about the person next to you? They have value and worth as well. What about the people who work with you? Even though they may be a pain in the ass at times, they have value and worth too. Now here's the rub that we don't like to think about: What about the homeless man under the bridge or the heroin addict? Believe it or not, they have value and worth too. Sometimes, law enforcement officers, as well as the general public, have a tendency to believe we are "above" other people – that they are scumbags and unworthy of anything. But in reality, we're *all* equal. If you told me 20 years ago that I would write the previous sentence, I would have laughed in your face again. It wasn't until I started to believe as a Christian that we were all truly created equal—that my view of my life and others changed. Each of us may have a different race, gender, social status, income level, education or job, but we are all equal.

Principle #2: Know That You Are Not Alone.

Whatever you may be feeling or experiencing, know that others have felt and experienced the same thing. When I was the Western New York Area Director for the American Foundation for Suicide Prevention (AFSP), I did a short talk in Buffalo, NY at a suicide prevention fundraiser. We were in a large park with a thousand attendees, most of who were suicide loss survivors. I asked the crowd to raise their hands if they had felt all alone, and that no one understood what they were going through when they lost their loved one to suicide. Every hand went up. Then I said, "Keep your hands up and look around you. You weren't alone then, and you're not alone now." It was an incredibly powerful moment.

Each of us has faced—and will face—situations and circumstances where we may feel alone and misunderstood. I believe that's the biggest reason most law enforcement officers hang out with other law enforcement officers. We understand one another. But do we really? What happens to us after "choir practice" when we go home to an empty house or apartment? After we laugh about a tragic incident using cop humor, what are we really experiencing in our minds when we lay our heads down on our pillows? How do we feel when our moms die, our kids won't talk to us, or our spouses leave us? When the dust settles on difficult events in our lives, law enforcement officers are human beings who feel very alone. We know we could be around 100 other people, but still feel all alone.

But we aren't. No matter how we feel, we must remind ourselves, as well as those we care about, that we're not alone. Others have experienced the same thing and survived. The feeling of being alone during a difficult time is horrible, so being open about what you're feeling, and being with people who demonstrate empathy and compassion (not just take you out for a beer or two) is important.

Principle #3: Be Honest with Yourself and Others.

Honesty about what is really happening in your life is key to sustaining emotional health, and undoubtedly one of the hardest principles on this list. As one might imagine, there's one person we need to be honest with first and foremost—the person we see in the mirror every morning. Looking at ourselves and looking inside ourselves is not always a pleasant experience. I certainly know that honesty wasn't easy for me, but I could not heal until I was truthful with myself. Throughout this book, I've discussed some difficult things. At times, it felt raw not only for you to read, but also for me to write. But I know this for a fact: If you're not honest with yourself, true emotional health will never happen. But the honesty principle doesn't end with you. The second part of the principle is to be honest with other people who love and care about you. Because of my lack of honesty with others, my life was riddled with guilt and shame that, combined with all my mental health issues, often drove me to severe thoughts of suicide.

People in your life will often ask, "How is your day? How are you doing?" The pat answer is usually, "Doing good" even when we're not doing very well at all. I have also noticed this exchange in other situations. When I was a pastor, people would come to Sunday services, and greeters would welcome them at the door. I would watch people as they were greeted and asked, "Hey, good morning. How are you?" The pat answer was always, "Doing good!" Since, like I said, I did the majority of pastoral counseling at the church, I would see people that I'd spoken with during the previous week give that pat answer. Yet, I knew that their spouse was cheating, their kids wouldn't talk with them, or they drank too much. I knew the "doing good" line couldn't have been further from the truth. Please understand that I am in no way telling you to be honest with every person who asks you how you're doing. Most people ask that question to be polite and probably don't really want to know the actual answer. However, if someone who truly cares about you asks that question, answering, "To be honest, I'm not doing very well," could open up your life to some real and healing conversations.

I've had my share of honest conversations with people about what was going on in my life over the years. I've admitted things and shared deep personal issues that I never thought I would. Having honest conversations certainly didn't happen overnight, and some things took years for me to open up about. But this I know—until we are willing to truly be honest with ourselves and with those who love us, we'll always be stuck. As I mentioned, this principle is not easy. Understanding that your life has value, and that you're not alone, will hopefully help you with being honest about what's happening within you.

Principle #4: Share with Others.

Sharing is more than simply being honest as described in Principle #3, and it can be just as hard. It's saying, "Hey honey, can I talk to you about something?" "Chief, do you have a few minutes to talk in the office?" "Sarge, do you mind if I sit down with you? Can I buy you a cup of coffee because I don't know where else to turn to?" It's reaching out to a professional to say, "I can't live like this anymore" or simply "Something's wrong." Sharing is one of the most helpful ways to understand what is causing distress so you can achieve and maintain emotional health.

Sharing professional issues such as trauma, or critical incidents, is often accomplished with fellow officers who have experienced the same thing. Remember Principle #2? You're not alone. If you are a police officer or supervisor, it's important to provide an open and safe environment where your fellow officers can talk with you. Some of this can be done through debriefing. In my day, like I've mentioned a few times, I don't think the words, "debriefing" or "peer-to-peer counseling" existed in law enforcement. Our culture didn't allow it. Often it still doesn't, but again, as I've mentioned many times, that's not working very well for us.

Lt. Jeremy Romo of the St. Louis County, Missouri Police Department, is an authority in his department on Critical Incident Stress Management (CISM). Here is his very clear explanation of what it is, why it is needed, and his own experiences. I personally believe that the last statement is a key reason for Principle #5. Sharing openly with others promotes positive coping skills and resiliency for the next time, and we know that there will always be a next time.

"I did not experience my first CISD until I was 15 years into my law enforcement career. This occurred after experiencing 5 months of civil unrest in Ferguson, Missouri from August to December 2014. After the dust began to settle from that historic event that changed the law enforcement profession forever, I, along with other members of my Police Department, could see the profound effect this event had on members of my agency. The civil unrest in Ferguson, MO was a 5-month extended critical incident for law enforcement officers in the St. Louis Area. The volunteer members of the St. Louis CISM Team conducted numerous POST Action Discussions over a month, to cover over 800 law enforcement officers. After experiencing the Post Action Discussion and seeing how beneficial it was to my fellow law enforcement officers, I applied and was accepted as a volunteer member of the Greater St. Louis CISM Team.

The word, "Debrief" can have many different meanings in different situations. A Critical Incident Stress Debriefing (CISD) for first responders is an interactive group process developed by Dr. Jeffrey Mitchell of the University of Maryland, Baltimore County, and used by the International Critical Incident Stress Foundation (ICISF). Critical Incident Stress Management (CISM) strategy is designed for homogenous groups who have all experienced a specific traumatic event. It is not a therapy session.

A critical characteristic of a CISD is that it is facilitated by properly trained team members, one of which is ideally a mental health professional. I believe it is best if that mental health professional is a former first responder or familiar with what it is like to be a first responder. Those facilitators that are first responder peers should understand that if they identify a participant who needs further assistance, their role is to steer that individual to the appropriate resources.

Confidentiality is absolutely necessary if a CISD is going to be successful. Confidentiality is such an important component of a successful CISD, that some states have passed laws to protect the confidentiality of CISD participants. Members of my police department that are members of the local CISM team will not facilitate CISD's for critical incidents that affect our agency personnel. This provides an added level of comfort to participants to reassure them that what they say will not be repeated outside of the CISD, and within the department.

Although there are differing opinions on whether a CISD should be mandatory after a critical incident, I firmly believe it is best to require all involved to attend. The rampant stigma that surrounds first responders seeking help for mental health issues undoubtedly prevents many first responders who are given a choice from attending a CISD. However, when you make it mandatory, the officer that wants to go but is concerned about how they will be perceived can avoid feeling ashamed. I have also seen repeatedly, those officers who don't feel like they need to participate in a CISD end up benefiting the most. In addition, I have observed that comments made by someone who would otherwise not have participated in the CISD are beneficial for others in the group.

According to ICISF, the goals of a CISD are to reduce the crisis response, help the group of first responders maintain their ability to effectively do their job and assist in the identification of members of the group that may need additional support. As a participant in a CISD after a critical incident, I have personally experienced how participating has helped me manage the normal physical and psychological effects that are common after experiencing an abnormal event. Managing those effects of crises are critical to my ability to be a good co-worker, family member and effectively serve the community.

One of the benefits of a CISD is that it normalizes how the first responder is feeling. For example, participants in a CISD may learn that it was not unusual for them to have trouble sleeping, eating and having flashbacks for an incident they experienced. In fact, others in the group often identify with similar signs and symptoms of experiencing a traumatic event, and it normalizes their feelings and reactions to the critical incident. The teaching phase of a CISD allows trained CISD facilitators to urge participants to avoid negative coping strategies, and promote coping strategies that create resilience. Promoting positive coping mechanisms and resiliency in first responders, makes them better equipped to handle future critical incidents that they will inevitably experience during their career."

If sharing in a professional setting can be difficult, sharing with others regarding personal issues has its own challenges. Over my years in professional counseling, I've talked about my dysfunctional childhood and family, marriages, anger, depression, obsessive thoughts and behaviors, traumas, and thoughts of suicide. It's been a journey to be sure. But if you recall, it all started with my statement to my second wife in 1995: "I need to talk with you about something." I was honest with myself and then shared with those around me and got professional help. It was hard, but it saved my life.

Principle #5: Search.

Search for what is causing the challenges you are facing and what is getting in the way of obtaining your optimum mental health. This may come easily for some, but be more difficult for others. Often, it takes working with a professional to understand your issues, challenges and factors. For example, there may be personal issues that need to be addressed and worked on, such as childhood or adult trauma, substance-use, or any other addictions or behaviors that have been mentioned. There may be professional challenges that need to be openly discussed, such as work hours or assignments. If you recall, cumulative stress is often the combination of work and non-work-related stressors, so you may need to search for reasons in both areas.

Or perhaps, there may be environmental factors that need to be explored, such as financial or physical health issues. Remember that depression and other mental illnesses are medical conditions, which is why medication works for so many. If so, a visit to your primary care physician may be in order. You may also be struggling with spiritual issues. Research has repeatedly shown that believing in something higher than ourselves, whatever that may mean to an individual, can be a key protective factor in helping to find emotional health. Again, I would be remiss if I didn't say that it was my newfound faith in God in 2000 that literally changed my life around.

Quite often, when we look for causes and we don't have to look any further than ourselves, we have a tendency to blame other people for our actions. But every time we point our finger at someone else, we have three fingers pointing back at us. At the end of the day, we need to take responsibility for ourselves and our own behaviors.

It's very important for me to note, however, that there is one circumstance where blaming yourself is completely misguided; that is the circumstance of being a victim of sexual assault. I say this because I know that there are many men and women out there, even in law enforcement and within their own families, that have been a victim, either as a child or even adult, of this horrific act. If you or your family members fall into this category of victimization, know that it was in no way your fault and that only the perpetrator is responsible, and if you have not already done so please seek professional help and personal healing.

Principle #6: Take Constructive Action.

We're all very good at taking negative actions. We react negatively throughout our lives by turning to alcohol or other substances, hanging out with the wrong people, or just pretending we don't have any problems. In contrast, developing a healthy lifestyle both mentally and physically, by finding a hobby or building healthy bodies, is an example of taking positive action. Identifying exactly what we are doing that is negatively affecting our life, and then replacing it with positive and healthy coping mechanisms and skills, is a crucial component of emotional health and stability. People can often benefit from medication, rehabilitation, talk therapy, self-help or a combination of these as a way of taking positive action. Whatever you choose, just choose something.

Principle #7: Look At How You Think

For many of us, thinking in terms of extremes becomes the way we look at our lives. This is called distorted thinking. When traumatic events happen, we think that way even more. Dr. David Burns, in his 1999 book, *The Feeling Good Handbook*, lists 10 common cognitive distortions[1]. As you read these thought distortions and my examples, try to identify which ones you may be experiencing:

1. **All-or-nothing thinking.** You see things in black and white categories. Things are either right or wrong. Gray areas don't exist.

2. **Overgeneralization**. You see a single negative event as a never-ending pattern of defeating statements like, "I'm totally worthless" or "Everyone hates me" that permeate your thoughts. Using words like, "always, everyone, and all of the time" can be examples of overgeneralization. I used to say these so often, that when I hear myself say them now, they stick out like a sore thumb and I quickly catch myself in what I'm saying.

3. **Mental filter.** Focusing on one negative event or comment creates a negative sense of reality. I know when I receive evaluations back from my trainings, I could have 99 people out of 100 say that it was the greatest thing they've ever seen, but I would fixate on the one person who said that they didn't care for it.

4. **Disqualifying the positive (or not celebrating it).** This means that no matter what positive and encouraging things are said to you, they just don't matter. This is incredibly common with depression. When you do something well and receive positive feedback, you respond with, "I could have done it better" or "Thanks, but...." People around you are telling you one thing, but you quickly dismiss it in lieu of creating a negative thought about yourself instead.

5. **Jumping to conclusions**. We rarely jump to conclusions that point to the positive. Instead of telling ourselves that we nailed a professional exam, we conclude that we are never going to get a promotion because we must have screwed up the test. We act like we are mind readers. I do this so often. If I don't get an e-mail from someone as soon as I think I should, I figure they must be mad at me. If someone doesn't call or text me back right away, they must not want to talk to me or want me in their life. We also act like fortune tellers. After a divorce, for example, we predict that nobody will ever love us again, instead of believing that someone out there will make our life better.

6. **Magnification or minimization**. You can exaggerate what you have done wrong or even look at someone else's achievements, and believe they are so much better than you. When I would review reports and call one of my officers over to correct something, I would often get the reaction of them thinking they couldn't do anything right.

7. **Emotional reasoning**. Our feelings lie to us, especially the negative ones. I feel like I have no friends, so I must not have any friends. I feel like someone laughed at me, so I must look stupid. I feel like someone disrespected me, so I need to get defensive. Our feelings quite often misinterpret reality.

8. **Should statements.** Our life is often riddled with, "Should-a, Could-a, Would-a." I know mine often is. Guilt, regrets, and remorse are common in human beings. In my classes I tell people not to 'should' all over people. Telling yourselves or others what you or they should have done, or should do in the future, can often lead to feelings of frustration, resentment, and even anger.

9. **Labeling and mislabeling.** "He's an idiot. They are all losers. I'm just a failure." are all labeling statements. Often, we label ourselves or others based on one single event or point in time, often what we did last. Remember Principle #1, that you and others have value and worth? Labeling or mislabeling yourself and others dismisses that entire principle.

10. **Personalization**: How many of us have apologized for something we had nothing to do with? I've said that I'm sorry it's raining, and I've apologized for someone else's behaviors. Many domestic violence victims do this. "It's my fault he hit me, because I didn't do the dishes." Taking on someone else's behavior or situations will lead you to believe that you are responsible for things you have no control over.

Many of us have experienced these ten distortions at some point in our lives. I know that I still do. If we have these thought distortions long enough, we start to believe them. If we are having a good day, they may not impact us very much. But if we are having a bad day, these thoughts creep into our minds and often do not go away very easily. Recognizing which ones we're having, and then actually working on replacing them with positive reflections of our lives, helps obtain and sustain good emotional health.

Some distorted thinking can simply be, "Woe is me. Here we go again. Another day of just trying to get through life" Many of us do this day after day. So often, I see someone I haven't seen in a while and ask, "Hey man, how are you doing? What's new?" All too often I get the response, "You know, same old shit, different day." I could see that same person five years from now and get the exact same response all over again. In a couple of years, I'll be turning 60. One thing that I have come to truly believe over my years on this earth—despite all my mental health issues, marriages, raising a family, traumas, hospitalizations, and suicide attempts—is that life should be more than just, "You know, same old shit, different day." Life is too short to live like that.

Principle #8: Know That Recovery Is Possible.

If I didn't believe that recovery is possible, I wouldn't have written this book. Principle #8 is the most important one of all. If someone doesn't believe in recovery and hope for a better life, they will prevent any true emotional health and healing from ever happening. People can and do get better. Mental illness and trauma related issues are treatable. Marriages can be healed. Lives can be saved. People with mental health issues can recover or manage their conditions and lead happy, healthy, productive lives. They contribute to society and make the world a better place.

I was asked once, "How can someone who's still mentally ill talk about recovery?" Recovery is a process, and it doesn't happen overnight. Recovery doesn't mean that everything has gone away or that you're all better. Recovery looks different for everyone because we're all different. If someone had told me back during my early hospitalizations, that I'd be traveling throughout the country speaking about mental illness and suicide, I would have thought they had more cognitive distortions than I did.

Emotional health—just like physical health—is important at every stage of life. It is important to every person we encounter throughout our life and career. Unfortunately, emotional health usually takes a back seat to everything else life throws at us. But without it, we will never recognize our worth. Be honest about what's happening in our lives. Be healthy enough to look at what's causing our stress. Be able to share our lives with others. Take positive measures for healthy growth. Identify our distorted thing. Understand that recovery and a better life are truly possible. That's what I believe, and that is what I have experienced.

CHAPTER 15

CHANGE IS NECESSARY

Change is hard. It takes time and requires consistency. In many ways, we have not changed how we understand, prevent, and treat suicide, trauma and mental illness in general. However, for those of us in law enforcement, how we look at our profession, society, one another, and life in general has stayed pretty much the same for a very long time. Here is what I believe from the bottom of my heart: Unless we are willing to make real and sustained changes in our law enforcement culture, and in our lives and families, and are not be able to overcome the darkness that can easily permeate our lives, someone else will be writing a book about this exact same subject 20 years from now.

Those changes can be in the form of:

- Yearly confidential mental health screenings.

- Offering trusted officer assistance programs and counseling.

- Developing and implementing a peer to peer program.

- Revising and updating outdated and stigmatizing fitness for duty policies.

- Providing real and professional debriefing for not only critical incidents, but for other forms of trauma that we don't view as 'critical', but that clearly take the same toll on officers.

- Departments removing the fear of being disciplined for having mental health issues and developing a culture of encouragement in seeking mental health treatment in their officers.

The stigmas we had in the past about mental illness really should no longer exist today. We have learned so much about mental health and trauma, but we need to re-examine how we respond to it. For law enforcement, that means change that affects everyone from recruits to high-level administration. Personally, I was lucky to have worked in an environment that was ahead of its time. Just imagine if I had been fired for being mentally ill and suicidal in 1996 when I sat ranting at my family and fellow officers from a locked bathroom in my home. My life would have turned out quite differently. More than likely, I would not be alive to write this book. Many others have not been as fortunate as me. I absolutely loved being a police officer, and believe it or not, I miss it every day. Even though I mentioned the many challenges that I, and others in our profession experience, I would take the test and get hired all over again if I could. But this time, I would do things much differently. None of us can change the past no matter how much we wish we could. All we can do is look towards the future of our profession.

Change starts with taking a hard look at our individual mindsets and our culture. It begins by understanding and openly discussing where we fall short, beginning with ourselves and those we love and who love us back. Change is activated by seeing ourselves as people who have the ability to shine the light on our humanity, no matter our profession, rank, social status, race, gender, or economic position.

As I've said to peers for a couple of decades, it's incredibly important to note that if you are dealing with any mental health issue whatsoever, you are still responsible for your behavior. We can easily blame someone else or a situation for how we're feeling, but at the end of the day we own our own recovery. We can seek treatment, therapy, medication, and more, but we must acknowledge that we are the only ones who can make our recovery actually happen.

Throughout this book, I have given specific examples of ways we can change in order to debunk the myths of mental illness, reduce suicides, manage stress and trauma, address PTSD, overcome addiction, and treat depression. I have talked about changes that are needed in family relationships. I have shared specific advice on how to change lives by promoting emotional health. I have also spent time talking about the vital need to end the silence and reduce the stressors in police culture that contribute to suicide, trauma, and mental illness.

So why is change so hard? At the risk of sounding cliché, emotional trauma does not bleed, so we have a tendency to ignore it. Even though the wounds are not visible, we forget that emotional wounds need the same attention, and quite often much more, than the physical traumas we endure. Let me illustrate this point with one last story.

During the winter of 1999, two of my officers—one whom had a recruit with them—responded to a domestic dispute at 3 a.m. The husband assaulted his wife, and the wife took a bottle and broke it over his head, causing him to bleed profusely. He was intoxicated, and as you might imagine, rather resistant. When the officers tried to arrest him, he put up a fight, and they called for assistance. I was first to pull up. As I walked toward the house, the man came charging out. As I put my hand out to stop him, he took a swing at me and connected on the left side of my head. Now we were fighting—off the sidewalk, back into the house, and in the foyer, which was a very small space. Each of us was trying to gain advantage over the other.

As we were punching, pulling, and turning, my right knee twisted, and I felt my knee pop. My ACL had torn severely, and I fell flat on my back into the living room. He fell on top of me, straddling my chest. I couldn't move or stand up as he began punching me in the face over and over with the blood from his cuts bleeding into my mouth, face, and eyes. I tried grabbing his hands and face to lessen the blows when I smelled mace in the air. Another officer was able to roll him off me and handcuff him. I got up on my good leg, went out to the front porch and leaned against the wall. My knee hurt so badly, and I started yelling and swearing rather loudly. I felt like my knee was broken in half. I was taken to the hospital where I was examined. A couple of weeks later, I had surgery and received pins in my knee to repair my ACL. During the many weeks of physical therapy, I would moan and groan from the pain. One of the lessons I took away from that incident was that fighting is very overrated, especially when you get older and lose one.

I have learned another more important lesson, however. I yelled about my injury because I was hurt and angry. I could scream in pain because that was acceptable. Everyone asked how I was and if I was okay. No one thought less of me, no one questioned my behavior. Contrast that with how I dealt with depression, trauma, and suicide for years. I kept my mouth shut. I didn't say anything to anyone, because of a deep and legitimate fear of what they would say and how they would see me. My mental state was way more debilitating than my knee and far more difficult to recover from, but I wrapped myself in silence, and it came close to killing me, over and over again.

After reading this book, it is my sincere hope that we all begin to look at ourselves and those around us a little differently; that we begin to know that it is okay to ask for help and just as important, to give it; that we begin to treat everyone around us with dignity, respect, and compassion. As I mentioned in the Preface of this book, I believe strongly that law enforcement is and will always be a noble profession, even when society and the media belittle it. Not everyone should be in it, and certainly not everyone can do it. We really are rather unique—neither better than anyone else nor below, but certainly unique. Let us always remind ourselves that in our culture, and more importantly in our lives, we can make a difference. In everything we do, everywhere we go, and in everything we say, personally and professionally, we will make a difference. However, it is up to each of us, if it is going to be a good difference or not so good a difference. We are literally the only ones who can make that happen. At the end of every class I do, whether it be for law enforcement or not, my ending slide reads, "In all encounters with those living with a mental health related issue, it is imperative to treat every individual with dignity, compassion, understanding, and respect." That goes for how we treat people we encounter, how we treat one another, and especially how we treat ourselves.

May God bless you always, keep you safe and bring you peace.

ENDNOTES

Introduction

1. "Law Enforcement Facts," National Law Enforcement Officers Memorial Fund, April 30, 2020, https://nleomf.org/facts-figures/law-enforcement-facts.
2. "Corrections Officer Jobs," How to Become a Correctional Officer (Strayer University, 2020), https://www.correctionalofficeredu.org/careers/.
3. Amy Chillag, "Every Year, 46 Million Americans Deal with Mental Illness. Only 41% Get Help. Here's How You Can.," CNN (Cable News Network, October 7, 2019), https://www.cnn.com/2019/05/08/health/iyw-how-to-get-mental-health-help/index.html.
4. "Suicide Statistics," American Foundation for Suicide Prevention, May 14, 2020, https://afsp.org/suicide-statistics/.
5. Accessed May 31, 2020, https://www.thenationalcouncil.org/wp-content/uploads/2013/05/Trauma-infographic.pdf?daf=375ateTbd56.

Chapter 3: The Cost of Silence

1. "Electroconvulsive Therapy (ECT)." Mayo Clinic. Mayo Foundation for Medical Education and Research, October 12, 2018. https://www.mayoclinic.org/tests-procedures/electroconvulsive-therapy/about/pac-20393894.

Chapter 5: Stressors and the Police Culture

1. Philip S. Wang, "Failure and Delay in Initial Treatment Contact After First Onset of Mental Disorders in the National Comorbidity Survey Replication," Archives of General Psychiatry (American Medical Association, June 1, 2005), https://jamanetwork.com/journals/jamapsychiatry/fullarticle/208684.
2. John G. Stratton, *Police Passages* (Manhattan Beach, CA, NY: Glennon Pub. Co., 1984).

3. "Sleep Deprivation: Causes, Symptoms, and Treatment," Medical News Today (MediLexicon International), accessed May 31, 2020, https://www.medicalnewstoday.com/articles/307334.
4. Jon Sheinberg, "Podcast Series: The Beat," Podcast Series: The Beat | COPS OFFICE, January 2020, https://cops.usdoj.gov/thebeat.
5. "Police Officers," Data USA (the Census Bureau , 2018), https://datausa.io/profile/soc/police-officers.

Chapter 6: Debunking the Stigma of Mental Illness

1. "Mental Health By the Numbers," NAMI (National Alliance on Mental Illness, 2020), https://www.nami.org/mhstats.
2. Samantha Gluck, "What Is Stigma?," HealthyPlace, 2020, https://www.healthyplace.com/stigma/stand-up-for-mental-health/what-is-stigma.
3. "Live Your Life Well," Mental Health America, 2020, https://mhanational.org/live-your-life-well.
4. "Mental Health Conditions," NAMI (National Alliance on Mental Illness, 2020), https://www.nami.org/learn-more/mental-health-conditions.
5. "Home: Mental Health First Aid Portal," Mental Health Instructor Portal (National Council for Behavioral Health), accessed June 2, 2020, https://instructors.mentalhealthfirstaid.org/adult-curriculum.
6. "Statistics," National Institute of Mental Health (U.S. Department of Health and Human Services), accessed June 2, 2020, https://www.nimh.nih.gov/health/statistics/index.shtml.
7. Philip S. Wang, "Failure and Delay in Initial Treatment Contact After First Onset of Mental Disorders in the National Comorbidity Survey Replication," Archives of General Psychiatry (American Medical Association, June 1, 2005), https://jamanetwork.com/journals/jamapsychiatry/fullarticle/208684.
8. David Z. Hambrick, "Bad News for the Highly Intelligent," Scientific American (Scientific American, December 5, 2017), https://www.scientificamerican.com/article/bad-news-for-the-highly-intelligent/.

Chapter 7: Understanding Depression

1. "Major Depression," National Institute of Mental Health (U.S. Department of Health and Human Services), accessed June 13, 2020, https://www.nimh.nih.gov/health/statistics/major-depression.shtml.

2. "Mental Health By the Numbers," NAMI, accessed June 3, 2020, https://www.nami.org/mhstats.

3. "Substance Abuse and Mental Health Issues," HelpGuide.org, accessed June 13, 2020, https://www.helpguide.org/articles/addictions/substance-abuse-and-mental-health.htm.

4. "Depression," NAMI, August 2017, https://www.nami.org/About-Mental-Illness/Mental-Health-Conditions/Depression/Treatment.

Chapter 8: Pathways of Stress and Trauma

1. Bing (Microsoft), accessed June 2, 2020, https://www.bing.com/search?q=definition+stress.

2. "Stress Management for Emergency Personnel," QuickSeries (QuickSeries Publishing, June 26, 2017), https://www.quickseries.com/products/stress-management-for-emergency-personnel-2/?query_search=Stress+Management+for+Emergency+Personnel.

3. "VA.gov: Veterans Affairs," How Common is PTSD in Adults?, September 13, 2018, https://www.ptsd.va.gov/understand/common/common_adults.asp.

4. "Helping the World's Heroes Reveal, Release, Reconnect," Vicarious Trauma Institute - Helping the World's Heroes to Reveal, Release, Reconnect, accessed June 2, 2020, https://vicarioustrauma.com/whatis.html.

5. Ellie Izzo and Vicki Carpel Miller, *Second-Hand Shock: Surviving & Overcoming Vicarious Trauma* (Scottsdale, AZ, AZ: Unhooked Books, 2018).

Chapter 9: Phases of Cumulative Stress

1. Jeffrey T. Mitchell and Grady P. Bray, *Emergency Services Stress: Guidelines for Preserving the Health and Careers of Emergency Services Personnel* (Englewood Cliffs, NJ: Brady Book, 1990).

2. Jenn Beach, "How to Worry Less: 90% of What You Fear Won't Happen," Lifehack (Lifehack, June 23, 2017), https://www.lifehack.org/606679/how-to-worry-less-90-of-what-you-fear-wont-happen.

3. Justin Fox et al., "Mental-Health Conditions, Barriers to Care, and Productivity Loss Among Officers in an Urban Police Department,"

Connecticut medicine (U.S. National Library of Medicine, 2012), https://pubmed.ncbi.nlm.nih.gov/23155671/.

4. Maurizio Pompili et al., "Suicidal Behavior and Alcohol Abuse," International journal of environmental research and public health (Molecular Diversity Preservation International (MDPI), April 2010), https://www.ncbi.nlm.nih.gov/pmc/articles/PMC2872355/.

Chapter 10: The Pain of PTSD

1. "https://www.veterans.gc.ca/," https://www.veterans.gc.ca/ §, accessed 2020, https://www.veterans.gc.ca/pdf/mental-health/ptsd_warstress_e.pdf.

2. "Posttraumatic Stress Disorder," NAMI, accessed June 13, 2020, https://www.nami.org/About-Mental-Illness/Mental-Health-Conditions/Posttraumatic-Stress-Disorder.

3. "VA.gov: Veterans Affairs," PTSD Basics, August 7, 2018, https://www.ptsd.va.gov/understand/what/ptsd_basics.asp.

4. Kathryn M Magruder et al., "Prevention and Public Health Approaches to Trauma and Traumatic Stress: a Rationale and a Call to Action," European journal of psychotraumatology (Co-Action Publishing, March 18, 2016), https://www.ncbi.nlm.nih.gov/pmc/articles/PMC4800286/.

Chapter 11: Overcoming Addiction and Compulsive Behavior

1. "Addiction," Merriam-Webster (Merriam-Webster), accessed June 9, 2020, https://www.merriam-webster.com/dictionary/addiction.

2. Ann Pietrangelo, "How to Identify and Treat a Pornography Addiction," Healthline (Healthline Media, June 7, 2019), https://www.healthline.com/health/pornography-addiction.

3. "Police and Addiction," Psychology Today (Sussex Publishers, March 30, 2018), https://www.psychologytoday.com/us/blog/sure-recovery/201803/police-and-addiction.

4. "Police and Addiction: Why Police Officers Are Nearly Three Times as Li," PRWeb, February 7, 2018, https://www.prweb.com/releases/2018/02/prweb15182365.htm.

5. "Global Status Report on Alcohol and Health 2018," World Health Organization (World Health Organization, August 21, 2019), https://www.who.int/substance_abuse/publications/global_alcohol_report/en/.

6. Arthur Hughes et al., "Prescription Drug Use and Misuse in the United States: Results from the 2015 National Survey on Drug Use and Health," Prescription Drug Use and Misuse in the United States: Results from the 2015 National Survey on Drug Use and Health, accessed June 10, 2020, https://www.samhsa.gov/data/sites/default/files/NSDUH-FFR2-2015/NSDUH-FFR2-2015.htm.

7. National Institute on Drug Abuse, "Summary of Misuse of Prescription Drugs," National Institute on Drug Abuse, April 13, 2020, https://www.drugabuse.gov/publications/research-reports/misuse-prescription-drugs/overview.

8. Jared Wadley, "College Students Say Nonmedical Use of ADHD Drugs Helps Them Study," University of Michigan News, December 16, 2008, https://news.umich.edu/college-students-say-nonmedical-use-of-adhd-drugs-helps-them-study/.

9. "What Is Food Addiction?," Food Addiction Institute, accessed June 10, 2020, https://foodaddictioninstitute.org/what-is-food-addiction/.

10. "Compulsive Sexual Behavior," Mayo Clinic (Mayo Foundation for Medical Education and Research, February 7, 2020), https://www.mayoclinic.org/diseases-conditions/compulsive-sexual-behavior/symptoms-causes/syc-20360434.

11. Mayo Clinic. "Compulsive Sexual Behavior."

12. Mara Tyler, "Recognizing an Addiction Problem," Healthline, January 12, 2018, https://www.healthline.com/health/addiction/recognizing-addiction.

13. "Home : Mental Health First Aid Portal," Mental Health Instructor Portal (National Council for Behavioral Health), accessed June 2, 2020, https://instructors.mentalhealthfirstaid.org/adult-curriculum.

Chapter 12: The Ultimate Consequence: Suicide

1. "Honoring the Service of Police Officers Who Died by Suicide," Blue H.E.L.P., May 2, 2020, https://bluehelp.org/.

2. "Report: 228 U.S. Law Enforcement Officers Died by Suicide in 2019 Law Enforcement Officer Deaths by Suicide Once Again Exceeded Line-of-Duty Deaths," StackPath, January 3, 2020, https://www.officer.com/command-hq/supplies-services/public-awareness/news/21119956/report-228-us-law-enforcement-officers-died-by-suicide-in-2019.
3. "Facts and Statistics," American Association of Suicidology, March 13, 2020, https://suicidology.org/facts-and-statistics/.
4. American Association of Suicidology, "Facts and Statistics."
5. Ibid.
6. Ibid
7. "Suicide Statistics," American Foundation for Suicide Prevention, May 14, 2020, https://afsp.org/suicide-statistics/.
8. American Foundation for Suicide Prevention, "Suicide Statistics,"
9. Ibid.
10. American Association of Suicidology, "Facts and Statistics."
11. Ibid.
12. Ibid.
13. American Foundation for Suicide Prevention, "Suicide Statistics,"
14. "Firearm Suicide in the United States." EverytownResearch.org, February 20, 2020. https://everytownresearch.org/firearm-suicide/.
15. Institute of Medicine (US) Committee on Pathophysiology and Prevention of Adolescent and Adult Suicide, "FIREARM AVAILABILITY AND SUICIDE," Suicide Prevention and Intervention: Summary of a Workshop. (U.S. National Library of Medicine, January 1, 1970), https://www.ncbi.nlm.nih.gov/books/NBK223849/.
16. American Association of Suicidology, "Facts and Statistics."
17. American Foundation for Suicide Prevention, "Suicide Statistics,"
18. American Association of Suicidology, "Facts and Statistics."
19. "Why Suicide Prevention Matters," LivingWorks, June 24, 2019, https://www.livingworks.net/why-suicide-prevention-matters.
20. "Law Enforcement," NAMI, 2020, https://www.nami.org/Advocacy/Crisis-Intervention/Law-Enforcement.
21. Indra Cidambi, "Police and Addiction," Psychology Today (Sussex Publishers, March 30, 2018), https://www.psychologytoday.com/us/blog/sure-recovery/201803/police-and-addiction.
22. Thomas Joiner, "The Interpersonal-Psychological Theory of Suicidal ...," https://www.apa.org/ (American Psychological

Association, June 2019), https://www.apa.org/science/about/psa/2009/06/sci-brief.

23. Traci Pedersen, "One-Third of Suicides Involve Heavy Alcohol Consumption," Psych Central, August 8, 2018, https://psychcentral.com/news/2014/06/21/one-third-of-suicides-involve-heavy-alcohol-consumption/71515.html.

24. Susan Freinkel, "Depression: The Secret Men Won't Admit," The Healthy (originally published in Reader's Digest, September 3, 2019), https://www.thehealthy.com/mental-health/depression/depression-in-men/.

25. "Depression & Mental Health Assessments - Primary Care and Specialist," AssessMD, accessed June 9, 2020, http://www.assessmd.com/primary-care-specialists.

Chapter 13: Shining the Light on Family

1. Alex Roslin and Susanna Hope, "Chapter 11, 'I Just Couldn't Walk Away,'" in *Police Wife: the Secret Epidemic of Police Domestic Violence* (Lac Brome, Québec: Sugar Hill Books, 2017), p. 134.

Chapter 14: Achieving and Maintaining Emotional Health

1. David D. Burns, *The Feeling Good Handbook* (Penguin, 1999).

BIBLIOGRAPHY

"Addiction." Merriam-Webster. Merriam-Webster. Accessed June 9, 2020. https://www.merriam-webster.com/dictionary/addiction.

Arthur Hughes, Matthew R. Williams, Rachel N. Lipari, and Jonaki Bose. Prescription Drug Use and Misuse in the United States: Results from the 2015 National Survey on Drug Use and Health. Accessed June 10, 2020. https://www.samhsa.gov/data/sites/default/files/NSDUH-FFR2-2015/NSDUH-FFR2-2015.htm.

Beach, Jenn. "How to Worry Less: 90% of What You Fear Won't Happen." Lifehack. Lifehack, June 23, 2017. https://www.lifehack.org/606679/how-to-worry-less-90-of-what-you-fear-wont-happen.

Bing. Microsoft. Accessed June 2, 2020. https://www.bing.com/search?q=definition stress.

Burns, David D. *The Feeling Good Handbook*. Penguin, 1999.

Chillag, Amy. "Every Year, 46 Million Americans Deal with Mental Illness. Only 41% Get Help. Here's How You Can." CNN. Cable News Network, October 7, 2019. https://www.cnn.com/2019/05/08/health/iyw-how-to-get-mental-health-help/index.html.

Cidambi, Indra. "Police and Addiction." Psychology Today. Sussex Publishers, March 30, 2018. https://www.psychologytoday.com/us/blog/sure-recovery/201803/police-and-addiction.

"Compulsive Sexual Behavior." Mayo Clinic. Mayo Foundation for Medical Education and Research, February 7, 2020. https://www.mayoclinic.org/diseases-conditions/compulsive-sexual-behavior/symptoms-causes/syc-20360434.

"Corrections Officer Jobs." How to Become a Correctional Officer. Strayer University, 2020. https://www.correctionalofficeredu.org/careers/.

"Depression & Mental Health Assessments - Primary Care and Specialist." AssessMD. Accessed June 9, 2020. http://www.assessmd.com/primary-care-specialists.

"Depression." NAMI. Accessed June 3, 2020. https://www.nami.org/About-Mental-Illness/Mental-Health-Conditions/Depression.

"Electroconvulsive Therapy (ECT)." Mayo Clinic. Mayo Foundation for Medical Education and Research, October 12, 2018. https://www.mayoclinic.org/tests-procedures/electroconvulsive-therapy/about/pac-20393894.

"Facts and Statistics." American Association of Suicidology, March 13, 2020. https://suicidology.org/facts-and-statistics/.

"Firearm Suicide in the United States." EverytownResearch.org, February 20, 2020. https://everytownresearch.org/firearm-suicide/.

Fox, Justin, Mayur M Desai, Karissa Britten, Georgina Lucas, Renee Luneau, and Marjorie S Rosenthal. "Mental-Health Conditions, Barriers to Care, and Productivity Loss Among Officers in an Urban Police Department." Connecticut medicine. U.S. National Library of Medicine, 2012. https://pubmed.ncbi.nlm.nih.gov/23155671/.

Freinkel, Susan. "Depression: The Secret Men Won't Admit." The Healthy. originally published in Reader's Digest, September 3, 2019. https://www.thehealthy.com/mental-health/depression/depression-in-men/.

"Global Status Report on Alcohol and Health 2018." World Health Organization. World Health Organization, August 21, 2019. https://www.who.int/substance_abuse/publications/global_alcohol_report/en/.

Gluck, Samantha. "What Is Stigma?" HealthyPlace, 2020. https://www.healthyplace.com/stigma/stand-up-for-mental-health/what-is-stigma.

Hambrick, David Z. "Bad News for the Highly Intelligent." Scientific American. Scientific American, December 5, 2017. https://www.scientificamerican.com/article/bad-news-for-the-highly-intelligent/.

"Helping the World's Heroes Reveal, Release, Reconnect." Vicarious Trauma Institute - Helping the World's Heroes to Reveal, Release, Reconnect. Accessed June 2, 2020. https://vicarioustrauma.com/whatis.html.

"Home: Mental Health First Aid Portal." Mental Health Instructor Portal. National Council for Behavioral Health. Accessed June 2, 2020. https://instructors.mentalhealthfirstaid.org/adult-curriculum.

"Honoring the Service of Police Officers Who Died by Suicide." Blue H.E.L.P., May 2, 2020. https://bluehelp.org/.

How to Manage Trauma. *Www.thenationalcouncil.org.* Accessed May 31, 2020. https://www.thenationalcouncil.org/wp-content/uploads/2013/05/Trauma-infographic.pdf?daf=375ateTbd56.

https://www.veterans.gc.ca/ §. Accessed 2020. https://www.veterans.gc.ca/pdf/mental-health/ptsd_warstress_e.pdf.

Institute of Medicine (US) Committee on Pathophysiology and Prevention of Adolescent and Adult Suicide. "FIREARM AVAILABILITY AND SUICIDE." Suicide Prevention and Intervention: Summary of a Workshop. U.S. National Library of Medicine, January 1, 1970. https://www.ncbi.nlm.nih.gov/books/NBK223849/.

Izzo, Ellie, and Vicki Carpel Miller. *Second-Hand Shock: Surviving & Overcoming Vicarious Trauma.* Scottsdale, AZ, AZ: Unhooked Books, 2018.

Joiner, Thomas. "The Interpersonal-Psychological Theory of Suicidal ..." https://www.apa.org/. American Psychological Association, June 2019. https://www.apa.org/science/about/psa/2009/06/sci-brief.

"Law Enforcement." NAMI, 2020. https://www.nami.org/Advocacy/Crisis-Intervention/Law-Enforcement.

"Law Enforcement Facts." National Law Enforcement Officers Memorial Fund, April 30, 2020. https://nleomf.org/facts-figures/law-enforcement-facts.

"Live Your Life Well." Mental Health America, 2020. https://mhanational.org/live-your-life-well.

Magruder, Kathryn M, Nancy Kassam-Adams, Siri Thoresen, and Miranda Olff. "Prevention and Public Health Approaches to Trauma and Traumatic Stress: a Rationale and a Call to Action." European journal of psychotraumatology. Co-Action Publishing, March 18, 2016. https://www.ncbi.nlm.nih.gov/pmc/articles/PMC4800286/.

"Major Depression." National Institute of Mental Health. U.S. Department of Health and Human Services. Accessed June 13, 2020. https://www.nimh.nih.gov/health/statistics/major-depression.shtml.

"Mental Health By the Numbers." NAMI. National Alliance on Mental Illness, 2020. https://www.nami.org/mhstats.

"Mental Health Conditions." NAMI. National Alliance on Mental Illness, 2020. https://www.nami.org/learn-more/mental-health-conditions.

Mitchell, Jeffrey T., and Grady P. Bray. *Emergency Services Stress: Guidelines for Preserving the Health and Careers of Emergency Services Personnel.* Englewood Cliffs, NJ: Brady Book, 1990.

National Institute on Drug Abuse. "Summary of Misuse of Prescription Drugs." National Institute on Drug Abuse, April 13, 2020. https://www.drugabuse.gov/publications/research-reports/misuse-prescription-drugs/overview.

Pedersen, Traci. "One-Third of Suicides Involve Heavy Alcohol Consumption." Psych Central, August 8, 2018. https://psychcentral.com/news/2014/06/21/one-third-of-suicides-involve-heavy-alcohol-consumption/71515.html.

Pietrangelo, Ann. "How to Identify and Treat a Pornography Addiction." Healthline. Healthline Media, June 7, 2019. https://www.healthline.com/health/pornography-addiction.

"Police and Addiction." Psychology Today. Sussex Publishers, March 30, 2018. https://www.psychologytoday.com/us/blog/sure-recovery/201803/police-and-addiction.

"Police and Addiction: Why Police Officers Are Nearly Three Times as Li." PRWeb, February 7, 2018. https://www.prweb.com/releases/2018/02/prweb15182365.htm.

"Police Officers." Data USA. the Census Bureau , 2018. https://datausa.io/profile/soc/police-officers.

Pompili, Maurizio, Gianluca Serafini, Marco Innamorati, Giovanni Dominici, Stefano Ferracuti, Giorgio D Kotzalidis, Giulia Serra, et al. "Suicidal Behavior and Alcohol Abuse." International journal of environmental research and public health. Molecular Diversity Preservation International (MDPI), April 2010. https://www.ncbi.nlm.nih.gov/pmc/articles/PMC2872355/.

"Posttraumatic Stress Disorder." NAMI. Accessed June 13, 2020. https://www.nami.org/About-Mental-Illness/Mental-Health-Conditions/Posttraumatic-Stress-Disorder.

"Report: 228 U.S. Law Enforcement Officers Died by Suicide in 2019 Law Enforcement Officer Deaths by Suicide Once Again Exceeded Line-of-Duty Deaths." StackPath, January 3, 2020. https://www.officer.com/command-hq/supplies-services/public-awareness/news/21119956/report-228-us-law-enforcement-officers-died-by-suicide-in-2019.

Roslin, Alex, and Susanna Hope. "Chapter 11, 'I Just Couldn't Walk Away.'" Essay. In *Police Wife: the Secret Epidemic of Police Domestic Violence*, 134. Lac Brome, Québec: Sugar Hill Books, 2017.

Sheinberg, Jon. "Podcast Series: The Beat." Podcast Series: The Beat | COPS OFFICE, January 2020. https://cops.usdoj.gov/thebeat.

"Sleep Deprivation: Causes, Symptoms, and Treatment." Medical News Today. MediLexicon International. Accessed May 31, 2020. https://www.medicalnewstoday.com/articles/307334.

"Statistics." National Institute of Mental Health. U.S. Department of Health and Human Services. Accessed June 2, 2020. https://www.nimh.nih.gov/health/statistics/index.shtml.

Stratton, John G. *Police Passages*. Manhattan Beach, CA, NY: Glennon Pub. Co., 1984.

"Stress Management for Emergency Personnel." QuickSeries. QuickSeries Publishing, June 26, 2017. https://www.quickseries.com/products/stress-management-for-emergency-personnel-2/?query_search=Stress Management for Emergency Personnel.

"Substance Abuse and Mental Health Issues." HelpGuide.org. Accessed June 13, 2020. https://www.helpguide.org/articles/addictions/substance-abuse-and-mental-health.htm.

"Suicide Statistics." American Foundation for Suicide Prevention, May 14, 2020. https://afsp.org/suicide-statistics/.

Tyler, Mara. "Recognizing an Addiction Problem." Healthline, January 12, 2018. https://www.healthline.com/health/addiction/recognizing-addiction.

"VA.gov: Veterans Affairs." How Common is PTSD in Adults?, September 13, 2018. https://www.ptsd.va.gov/understand/common/common_adults.asp.

"VA.gov: Veterans Affairs." PTSD Basics, August 7, 2018. https://www.ptsd.va.gov/understand/what/ptsd_basics.asp.

Wadley, Jared. "College Students Say Nonmedical Use of ADHD Drugs Helps Them Study." University of Michigan News, December 16, 2008. https://news.umich.edu/college-students-say-nonmedical-use-of-adhd-drugs-helps-them-study/.

Wang, Philip S. "Failure and Delay in Initial Treatment Contact After First Onset of Mental Disorders in the National Comorbidity Survey Replication." Archives of General Psychiatry. American Medical Association, June 1, 2005. https://jamanetwork.com/journals/jamapsychiatry/fullarticle/208684.

"What Is Food Addiction?" Food Addiction Institute. Accessed June 10, 2020. https://foodaddictioninstitute.org/what-is-food-addiction/.

"Why Suicide Prevention Matters." LivingWorks, June 24, 2019. https://www.livingworks.net/why-suicide-prevention-matters.